Xiaolu Guo was born in 1973 in a fishing village in south China. She studied film at Beijing Film Academy, and worked as a screenwriter and film teacher. Xiaolu moved to London in 2002, where she began a diary written in English which became the seed for this novel. She divides her time between Europe and China.

A CONCISE CHINESE-ENGLISH DICTIONARY FOR LOVERS

Written in (deliberately bad) English, this romantic comedy is about two lovers who don't speak each other's language. Z has come to London to study. She calls herself Z because English people can't pronounce her name — but when she arrives at Heathrow she's no better at their language. When she winds up lodging with a Chinese family in Tottenham, she feels that she might as well not have left home. But then she meets a man who changes everything . . . Z enters a new world of sex, freedom and self-discovery. However, she learns that in the West, 'Love' does not always mean the same as in China — and you can master the English language but still not understand your man.

XIAOLU GUO

A CONCISE CHINESE-ENGLISH DICTIONARY FOR LOVERS

Complete and Unabridged

CHARNWOOD
Leicester

First published in Great Britain in 2007 by
Chatto & Windus
The Random House Group Limited
London

First Charnwood Edition
published 2007
by arrangement with
Chatto & Windus
The Random House Group Limited
London

British Library CIP Data

Guo, Xiaolu, 1973 –
A concise Chinese-English dictionary for lovers.—
Large print ed.—
Charnwood library series
1. Chinese—England—London—Fiction
2. Language and languages—Fiction
3. Intercultural communication—Fiction
4. Love stories 5. Large type books
I. Title
823.9'2 [F]

ISBN 978–1–84617–921–1

Published by
F. A. Thorpe (Publishing)
Anstey, Leicestershire

Set by Words & Graphics Ltd.
Anstey, Leicestershire
Printed and bound in Great Britain by
T. J. International Ltd., Padstow, Cornwall

This book is printed on acid-free paper

Text design by Dinah Drazin with contributions from Juliet Brooke and Harrison John Smith

For the man who lost my manuscript in Copenhagen airport, and knows how a woman lost her language.

Nothing in this book is true,
except for the love between her and him.

'What are you thinking?'

Usually the man says a thing, and the woman questions it. Their conversation goes like this:

HER: 'What are you thinking?'
HIM: 'Nothing'
HER: 'But what it is going on in your head?'
HIM: 'I feel sad about my life.'
HER: 'Why?'
HIM: 'Everything feels empty and endless.'
HER: 'What you want then?'
HIM: 'I want to find happiness.'
HER: 'You can't have happiness at all times. Sometimes you will be sad. Don't you think?'
HIM: 'But I don't see any happiness in my life.'
HER: 'Then what's your most near happiness?'
HIM: ' . . . The sea.'

Before

Sorry of my english

prologue

prologue n introduction to a play or book

Now.
    Beijing time 12 clock midnight.
    London time 5 clock afternoon.
    But I at neither time zone. I on airplane. Sitting on 25,000 km above to earth and trying remember all English I learning in school.
    I not met you yet. You in future.

        ★   ★   ★

Looking outside the massive sky. Thinking air staffs need to set a special time-zone for long-distance airplanes, or passengers like me very confusing about time. When a body floating in air, which country she belonging to?
    People's Republic of China passport bending in my pocket.

Passport type	**P**
Passport No.	**G00350124**
Name in full	**Zhuang Xiao Qiao**
Sex	**Female**
Date of birth	**23 JULY 1979**
Place of birth	**Zhe Jiang, P. R. China**

I worry bending passport bring trouble to immigration officer, he might doubting passport is fake and refusing me into the UK, even with noble word on the page:

China further and further, disappearing behind clouds. Below is ocean. I from desert town. Is the first time my life I see sea. It look like a dream.

As I far away from China, I asking me why I coming to West. Why I must to study English like parents wish? Why I must to get diploma from West? I not knowing what I needing. Sometimes I not even caring what I needing. I not caring if I speaking English or not. Mother only speaking in village dialect and even not speaking official Mandarin, but she becoming rich with my father, from making shoes in our little town. Life OK. Why they want changing my life?

And how I living in strange country West alone? I never been to West. Only Western I seeing is man working in Beijing British Embassy behind tiny window. He stamp visa on brand new passport.

What else I knowing about West? American TV series dubbing into Chinese, showing us big houses in suburb, wife by window cooking and car arriving in front house. Husband back work. Husband say Honey I home, then little childrens running to him, see if he bringing gift.

But that not my life. That nothing to do with my life. I not having life in West. I not having home in West. I scared.

I no speaking English.

I fearing future.

February

alien

alien *adj* foreign; repugnant (to); from another world *n* foreigner; being from another world

Is unbelievable, I arriving London, 'Heathlow Airport'. Every single name very difficult remembering, because just not 'London Airport' simple way like we simple way call 'Beijing Airport'. Everything very confuse way here, passengers is separating in two queues.

Sign in front of queue say: ALIEN and NON ALIEN.

I am alien, like Hollywood film *Alien*, I live in another planet, with funny looking and strange language.

I standing in most longly and slowly queue with all aliens waiting for visa checking. I feel little criminal but I doing nothing wrong so far. My English so bad. How to do?

In my text book I study back China, it says English peoples talk like this:

'*How are you?*'

'*I am very well. How are you?*'

'*I am very well.*'

Question and answer exactly the same!

Old saying in China: '*Birds have their bird language, beasts have their beast talk*' (鸟有鸟语，兽有兽言). English they totally another species.

9

Immigration officer holding my passport behind his accounter, my heart hanging on high sky. Finally he stamping on my visa. My heart touching down like air plane. Ah. Wo. Ho. Ha. Picking up my luggage, now I a legal foreigner. Because legal foreigner from Communism region, I must re-educate, must match this capitalism freedom and Western democracy.

All I know is: I not understanding what people say to me at all. From now on, I go with *Concise Chinese-English Dictionary* at all times. It is red cover, look just like *Little Red Book*. I carrying important book, even go to the toilet, in case I not knowing the words for some advanced machine and need checking out in dictionary. Dictionary is most important thing from China. *Concise* meaning simple and clean.

hostel

hostel n building providing accommodation at a low cost for a specific group of people such as students, travellers, homeless people, etc

First night in 'hostel'. Little *Concise Chinese-English Dictionary* hostel explaining: a place for 'people such as students, travellers and homeless people' to stay. Sometimes my dictionary absolute right. I am student and I am homeless looking for place to stay. How they knowing my situation *precisely?*

Thousands of additional words and phrases reflect scientific and technological innovations, as well as changes in politics, culture, and society. In particular, many new words and expressions as well as new usages and meanings which have entered the Chinese language as a result of China's open-door policy over the last decade have been included in the Chinese-English section of the dictionary.

That is sentence in *Preface*. All sentence in preface long like this, very in-understandable. But I must learning this stylish English because it high-standard English from authority. Is parents' command on me: studying how speak

11

and write English in England, then coming back China, leaving job in government work unit and making lots money for their shoes factory by big international business relations. Parents belief their life is dog's life, but with money they save from last several years, I make better life through Western education.

Anyway, *hostel* called 'Nuttington House' in Brown Street, nearby Edward Road and Baker Street. I write all the names careful in notebook. No lost. Brown Street seem really brown with brick buildings everywhere. Prison looking. Sixteen pounds for per bed per day. With sixteen pounds, I live in top hotel in China with private bathroom. Now I must learn counting the money and being mean to myself and others. Gosh.

★   ★   ★

First night in England is headache.

Pulling large man-made-in-China-suitcase into *hostel*, second wheel fall off by time I open the door. (First wheel already fall off when I get suitcase from airport's luggage bell.) Is typical suitcase produced by any factory in Wen Zhou, my hometown. My hometown China's biggest home-products industry town, our government says. Coat hangers, plastic washbasins, clothes, leather belts and nearly-leather bags, computer components etc, we make there. Every family in my town is factory. Big factories export their products to everywhere in the world, just like my parents get order from Japan, Singapore and

12

Israel. But anyway, one over-the-sea trip and I lost all the wheels. I swear I never buy any products made from home town again.

Standing middle of the room, I feeling strange. This is *The West*. By window, there hanging old red curtain with holes. Under feet, old blood-red carpet has suspicions dirty spots. Beddings, they covering by old red blanket too. Everything is dirty blood red.

Room smelling old, rotten. Suddenly my body feeling old too. 'English people respect history, not like us,' teachers say to us in schools. Is true. In China now, all buildings is no more than 10 years old and they already old enough to be demolished.

With my enormous curiosity, walking down to the night street. First night I away home in my entirely twenty-three years life, everything scare me. Is cold, late winter. Windy and chilli. I feeling I can die for all kinds of situation in every second. No safety in this country, I think unsafe feeling come from I knowing nothing about this country. I scared I in a big danger.

I scared by cars because they seems coming from any possible directing. I scared by long hair black man passing because I think he beating me up just like in films. I scared by a dog. Actually chained with old lady but I thinking dog maybe have mad-dog-illness and it suddenly bite me and then I in hospital then I have no money to pay and then I sent back to China.

Walking around like a ghost, I see two rough mans in corner suspicionly smoke and exchange

13

something. Ill-legal, I have to run — maybe they desperate drug addictors robbing my money. Even when I see a beggar sleeping in a sleep bag I am scared. Eyes wide open in darkness staring at me like angry cat. What he doing here? I am taught everybody in West has social security and medical insurance, so, why he needs begging?

I going back quickly to Nuttington House. Red old carpet, red old curtain, red old blanket. Better switch off light.

Night long and lonely, staying nervously in tacky room. London should be like emperor's city. But I cannot feel it. Noise coming from other room. Laughing in drunkenly way. Upstairs TV news speaking intensely nonsense. Often the man shouting like mad in the street. I worry. I worry I getting lost and nobody in China can find me anymore. How I finding important places including Buckingham Palace, or Big Stupid Clock? I looking everywhere but not seeing big posters of David Beckham, Spicy Girls or President Margaret Thatcher. In China we hanging them everywhere. English person not respect their heroes or what?

No sleeping. Switching on the light again. Everything turning red. Bloody new world. I study little red dictionary. English words made only from twenty-six characters? Are English a bit lazy or what? We have fifty thousand characters in Chinese.

Starting at page one:

A

Abacus: (meaning a wooden machine used for counting)

Abandon: (meaning to leave or throw away)

Abashed: (meaning to feel embrassed or regretful),

Abattoir: (meaning a place to kill the animals)

Abbess: (meaning the boss of woman monk's house)

Abbey: (meaning a temple)

Abbot: (meaning the boss of a temple)

Abbreviate: (meaning to write a word quickly)

Abduct: (meaning to tie somebody up and take away to somewhere)

Words becoming blurred and no meaning. The first night I falling into darkness with the jet-lag tiredness.

full english breakfast

1. Builder's Super Platter:
double egg, beans, bacon, sausage, bubble, mushroom, tomato, 2 toast, tea or coffee included.

2. Vegetarian Breakfast:
double egg, bubble, mushroom, beans, veggie sausage, hash browns, tea or coffee included.

'Talk doesn't cook rice,' say Chinese. Only thing I care in life is eating. And I learning English by food first, of course. Is most practical way.

Getting up early, I have free *Full English Breakfast* from my *hostel*. English so proud they not just say *hotel*, they say *Bed and Breakfast*, because breakfast so importantly to English situation. Even say 'B and B' everyone know what thinking about. Breakfast more important than Bed.

I never seeing a *breakfast* like that. Is big lunch for construction worker! I not believe every morning, my *hostel* offering everybody this meal, lasting three hours, from 7 clock to 10 clock. Food like messy scrumpled eggs, very salty bacons, burned bread, very thick milk, sweet bean in orange sauce, coffee, tea, milk, juice. Church or temple should be like this, giving the generosity to normal people. But 8.30 in the morning I refuse accepting two oily sausage, whatever it made by pork or by vegetables, is just

16

too fat for a little Chinese.

What is this 'baked beans'? White colour beans, in orange sticky sweet sauce. I see some baked bean tins in shop when I arrive to London yesterday. Tin food is very expensive to China. Also we not knowing how to open it. So I never ever try tin food. Here, right in front of me, this baked beans must be very expensive. Delicacy is baked beans. Only problem is, tastes like somebody put beans into mouth but spit out and back into plate.

Sitting on breakfast table, my belly is never so full. Still two pieces of bread and several 'baked tomatoes' on my plate. I can't chew more. Feeling guilty and wasty, I take out little *Concise Chinese-English Dictionary* from my pocket, start study English. My language school not starting yet, so I have to learn by myself first. Old Chinese saying: 'the stupid bird should fly first before other birds start to fly' (笨鸟先飞).

When I am studying the word *Accommodate*, woman come clean table, and tell me I must leave. She must hate me that I eat too much food here. But not my fault.

First morning, I steal white coffee cup from table. Second morning, I steal glass. So now in my room I can having tea or water. After breakfast I steal breads and boiled eggs for lunch, so I don't spending extra money on food. I even saving bacons for supper. So I saving bit money from my parents and using for cinema or buying books.

Ill-legal. I know. Only in this country three days and I already become thief. I never steal

17

piece of paper in own country. Now I studying hard on English, soon I stealing their language too.

Nobody know my name here. Even they read the spelling of my name: *Zhuang Xiao Qiao*, they have no idea how saying it. When they see my name starts from 'Z', stop trying. I unpronouncable Ms Z.

First three days in this country, wherever I walk, the voice from my parents echo my ears:

'*No talking strangers.*'

'*No talking where you live.*'

'*No talking how much money you have.*'

'*And most important thing: no trusting anybody.*'

That my past life. Life before in China. The warns speaking in my mother's harsh local dialect, of course, translation into English by *Concise Chinese-English Dictionary*.

properly

proper adj real or genuine; suited to a particular purpose; correct in behaviour; excessively moral

Today my first time taking taxi. How I find important place with bus and tube? Is impossibility. Tube map is like plate of noodles. Bus route is in-understandable. In my home town everyone take cheap taxi, but in London is very expensive and taxi is like the Loyal family look down to me.

Driver say: 'Please shut the door properly!'

I already shut the door, but taxi don't moving.

Driver shout me again: 'Shut the door properly!' in a *concisely* manner.

I am bit scared. I not understanding what is this 'properly'.

'I beg your pardon?' I ask. 'What is *properly?*'

'Shut the door properly!' Taxi driver turns around his big head and neck nearly break because of anger.

'But what is 'properly', Sir?' I so frightened that I not daring ask it once more again.

Driver coming out from taxi, and walking to door. I think he going kill me.

He opens door again, smashing it back to me hardly.

'Properly!' he shout.

★   ★   ★

Later, I go in bookshop and check 'properly' in *Collins English Dictionary* ('THE AUTHORITY ON CURRENT ENGLISH'). *Properly* means 'correct behaviour'. I think of my behaviour with the taxi driver ten minutes ago. Why incorrect? I go to accounter buy little *Collins* for my pocket

My small *Concise Chinese-English Dictionary* not having 'properly' meaning. In China we never think of 'correct behaviour' because every behaviour correct.

I want write these newly learned words everyday, make my own dictionary. So I learn English fast. I write down here and now, in every second and every minute when I hear a new noise from an English's mouth.

fog

fog n mass of condensed water vapour in the lower air, often greatly reducing visibility

'London is the Capital of fog.' It saying in middle school textbook. We studying chapter from Charles Dickens's novel *Foggy City Orphan*. Everybody know Oliver Twist living in city with bad fog. Is very popular novel in China.

As soon as I arriving London, I look around the sky but no any fogs. 'Excuse me, where I seeing the fogs?' I ask policeman in street.

'Sorry?' he says.

'I waiting two days already, but no fogs,' I say.

He just look at me, he must no understanding of my English.

When I return Nuttington House from my tourism visiting, reception lady tell me: 'Very cold today, isn't it?' But why she tell me? I know this information, and now is too late, because I finish my tourism visiting, and I wet and freezing.

Today I reading not allowed to stay more than one week in hostel. I not understanding hostel's policy. 'Money can buy everything in capitalism country' we told in China. My parents always saying if you have money you can make the devil push your grind stone.

But here you not staying even if you pay. My parents wrong.

I checking all cheap flats on LOOT in Zone 1 and 2 of London and ringing agents. All agents sound like from Arabic countries and all called Ali. Their English no good too. One Ali charges Marble Arch area; one Ali charges Baker Street area. But I meet different Alis at Oxford Circus tube station, and see those houses. I dare not to move in. Places dirty and dim and smelly. How I live there?

London, by appearance, so noble, respectable, but when I follow these Alis, I find London a refuge camp.

beginner

beginner n person who has just started learning to do something

Holborn. First day studying my language school. Very very frustrating.

'My name is Margaret Wilkinson, but please call me Margaret,' my grammar teach tells in front blackboard. But I must give respect, not just call Margaret. I will call Mrs Margaret.

'What is grammar? Grammar is the study of the mechanics and dynamics of language,' Mrs Margaret says in the classroom.

I not understanding what she saying. Mrs Margaret have a neatly cut pale blonde hair, with very serious clothes. Top and her bottom always same colour. She not telling her age, but I guessing she from 31 to 56. She wearing womans style shoes, high heel black leather, very possible her shoes are all made in home town Wen Zhou, by my parents. She should know it, one day I tell her. So she not so proud in front of us.

Chinese, we not having grammar. We saying things simple way. No verb-change usage, no tense differences, no gender changes. We bosses of our language. But, English language is boss of English user.

Mrs Margaret teaching us about nouns. I

discovering English is very scientific. She saying *nouns* have two types — countable and uncountable.

'You can say *a car*, but not *a rice*,' she says. But to me, *cars* are really uncountable in the street, and we can count the *rice* if we pay great attention to a rice bowl.

Mrs Margaret also explaining nouns is plural and singular.

'Jeans are pairs,' she says. But, everybody know jeans or trousers always one thing, you can't wear many jean or plural trouser. Four years old baby know that. Why waste ink adding 's'? She also saying nouns is three different gender: masculine, feminine, and neuter.

'A table is neuter,' she says.

But, who cares a table is neuter? Everything English so scientific and problematic. Unlucky for me because my science always very bad in school, and I never understanding mathematics. First day, already know I am *loser*.

After lunch breaking, Mrs Margaret introducing us little about verbs. Gosh, verb is just crazy. Verb has verbs, verbed and verb-ing. And verbs has three types of mood too: indicative, imperative, subjunctive. Why so moody? 'Don't be too frustrated. You will all soon be speaking the Queen's English.' Mrs Margaret smiles to me.

pronoun

pronoun n word, such as she or it, used to replace a noun

First week in language school, I speaking like this:

'Who is her name?'

'It costing I three pounds buying this disgusting sandwich.'

'Sally telling I that her just having coffee.'

'Me having fried rice today.'

'Me watching TV when me in China.'

'Our should do things together with the people.'

Always the same, the people laughing as long as I open my mouth.

'Ms Zh-u-ang, you have to learn when to use *I* as the subject, and when to use *me* as the object!'

Mrs Margaret speaking Queen's English to me.

So *I* have two *mes*? According to Mrs Margaret, one is subject *I* one is object *I*? But I only one I. Unless Mrs Margaret talking about incarnation or after life.

She also telling me I disorder when speaking English. Chinese we starting sentence from concept of *time* or *place*. Order like this:

Last autumn on the Great Wall we eat barbecue.

So time and space always bigger than little human in our country. Is not like order in English sentence, 'I', or 'Jake' or 'Mary' by front of everything, supposing be most important thing to whole sentence.

★   ★   ★

English a sexist language. In Chinese no 'gender definition' in sentence. For example, Mrs Margaret says these in class:

'Everyone must do *his* best.'

'If a pupil can't attend the class, he should let *his* teacher know.'

'We need to vote for a *chairman* for the student union.'

Always talking about mans, no womans!

Mrs Margaret later telling verb most difficult thing for our oriental people. Is not only 'difficult', is 'impossibility'! I not understanding why verb can always changing.

★   ★   ★

One day I find a poetry by William Shakespeare on school's library shelf. I studying hard. I even not stopping for lunch. I open little *Concise Dictionary* more 40 times checking new words. After looking some Shakespeare poetry, I will can return back my China home, teaching everyone about Shakespeare. Even my father know Shakespeare big dude, because our in our

26

local government evening classes they telling everyones Shakespeare most famous person from Britain.

One thing, even Shakespeare write bad English. For example, he says 'Where go thou?'. If I speak like that Mrs Margaret will tell me wrongly. Also I finding poem of him call 'An Outcry Upon Opportunity':

> 'Tis thou that execut'st the traitor's treason;
> Thou sett'st the wolf where he the lamb may get

I not understanding at all. What this ''tis', 'execut'st' and 'sett'st'? Shakespeare can writing that, my spelling not too bad then.

★ ★ ★

After grammar class, I sit on bus and have deep thought about my new language. Person as dominate subject, is main thing in an English sentence. Does it mean West culture respecting individuals more? In China, you open daily newspaper, title on top is 'OUR HISTORY DECIDE IT IS TIME TO GET RICH' or 'THE GREAT COMMUNIST PARTY HAVE THIRD MEETING' or 'THE 2008 OLYMPICS NEED CITIZENS PLANT MORE GREENS'. Look, no subjects here are mans or womans. Maybe Chinese too shaming putting their name first, because that not modest way to be.

slogan

slogan n catchword or phrase used in politics or advertising

I go in bookshop buy the English version of *Little Red Book*. Not easy read but very useful argue with English using Chairman Mao *slogans*. English version is without translator name on cover. Yes, no second name can be shared on Mao's work. Chairman Mao

has inherited, defended and developed Marxism-Leninism with genius, creatively and comprehensively and has brought it to a higher and completely new stage.

The English translators of this book, they are like feather compare with Tai Mountain.

In West, Mao's words work for me, though they not work in China now. Example, today big confusion in streets. Everywhere people marching to say no to war in Iraq.

'No war for oil!'

'Listen to your people!'

The demon-strators from everywhere in Britain, socialists, Communists, teachers, students, housewifes, labour workers, Muslim womans covered under the scarf with their children . . . They marching to the Hyde park. I am in march because I not finding way to hostel. So no choice except following. I search Chinese faces in the march team. Very few. Maybe they busy and desperately earning money in those Chinese Takeaways.

People in march seems really happy. Many smiles. They feel happy in sunshine. Like having weekend family picnic. When finish everyone rush drink beers in pubs and ladies gather in tea houses, rub their sore foots.

Can this kind of demon-stration stop war?

From Mao's little red book, I learning in school:

A revolution is not a dinner party, or writing an essay, or painting a picture, or doing embroidery; it cannot be so refined, so leisurely and gentle, so temperate, kind, courteous, restrained and magnanimous. A revolution is an insurrection, an act of violence with which one class overthrows another.

Probably Communist love war more than anybody. From Mao's opinion, war able be 'Just' although it is bloody. (But blood happen everyday anyway . . .) He say:

Oppose unjust war with just war, whenever possible.

29

So if people here want to against war in Iraq, they needing have civil war with their Tony Blair here, or their Bush. If more people bleeding in native country, then those mens not making war in other place.

weather

weather n day-to-day atmospheric conditions of a place v (cause to) be affected by the weather; come safely through

weather n the state of the atmosphere at a place and time in terms of temperature, wind, rain, etc

Carrying meat ball and pork slice from supermarket, now I am in place calling *Ye Olde English Tea Shop*. What is this 'Ye'? Why 'Olde' not 'Old'? Wrong spelling.

Tea house like Qing dynasty old style building waiting for being demolish. Everything looking really old here, especial wood stick beam in middle of house, supporting roof. Old carpet under the foot is very complication flower pattern, like something from emperor mother house.

'Where would you like to sit?', 'What can I get you?', 'A table for one person?', 'Are you alone?'. Smiling waiter ask so many questions. He making me feel bit lonely. In China I not have loneliness concept. Always we with family or crowd. But England, always alone, and even waiter always remind you you are alone . . .

Everybody listening the weather at this moment in tea house. All time in London, I hearing weather report from radios. It tells weather situation like emergency typhoon coming. But no emergency coming here. I checking *Concise Chinese-English Dictionary*. It saying all English *under the weather*, and all English is *weather beaten*, means uncomfortable. Is reasonable, of course. England everybody beaten by the weather. Always doubt or choice about weather. Weather it rain or weather it sunshine, you just not know.

Weather report also very difficult understand. The weather man not saying 'rain' or 'sunny' because they speaking in complication and big drama way. He reporting weather like reporting big war: 'Unfortunately . . . Hopefully . . . '. I listen two hours radio I meet twice weather report. Do they think British Empire as big China that it need to report at any time? Or clouds in this country changing every single minute? Yes, look at the clouds now, they are so suspicious! Not like my home town, often several weeks without one piece cloud in sky and weather man has nothing more to say. Some days he just saying 'It is Yin', which mean weather is negative.

confusion

confuse v mix up; perplex, disconcert; make unclear

English food very confusing. They eating and drinking strange things. I think even Confucius have great confusion if he studying English.

It is already afternoon about 3 o'clock and I so hungry. What can I eat, I asking waiter. He offering 'Afternoon Tea'. What? Eat afternoon tea?

So he showing me blackboard, where is a menu:

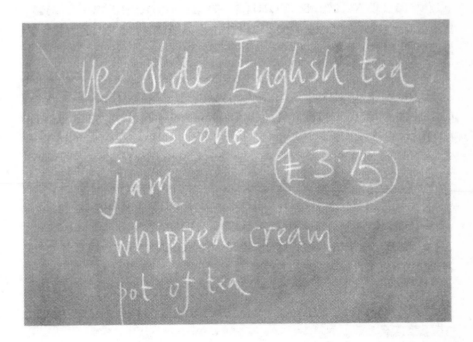

Whatever, I must to eat whatever they have or I faint. Three minutes later my thing arrives: 'scones' hot and thick and dry, cream is unbelieveable, butter is greasy, and jam are three kinds: raspberry, cramberry and strawberry. A white tea pot with a white tea cup.

I confusing again when I look at 'whipped cream' on little blackboard. What is that mean? How people whip the cream? I see a poster somewhere near Chinatown. On poster naked woman only wears leather boots and leather pants, and she whipping naked man kneeling down under legs. So a English chef also whipping in kitchen?

I put scones into mouth, and drink tea like horse. Next door me, I hearing somebody wanting 'frothy coffee'.

A lady with a young man. She say: 'Can I have a frothy coffee, please? And my friend will have a black coffee, with skimmed milk.'

It must be big work making something 'skimmed', and 'frothy', and 'whipped'. Why drinking become so complicating and need so much work?

And water are even more complicating here. Maybe raining everyday here and too much water so English making lots kind water.

I thirsty from eating dry scones.

Waiter asks me: 'What would you like? Still water, or filthy water?'

'What? Filthy water?' I am shocked.

'OK, filthy water.' He leave and fetch bottle of water.

I so curious about strange water. I opening bottle, immediately lots bubbles coming out. How they putting bubbles in water? Must be highly technicaled. I drinking it. Taste bitter, very filthy, not natural at all, like poison.

homesick

homesick adj sad because missing one's home and family

In my language school, Mrs Margaret ask me:
'Would you like some tea?'
'No,' I say.
She looking at me, her face suddenly frozen. Then she asking me again:
'Would you like some coffee then?'
'No. I don't want.'
'Are you sure you don't want anything?'
'No. I don't want anything wet,' I saying loudly, precisely.
Mrs Margaret looking very upset.
But why she asking me again and again? I already answer her from first time.
'Oh, dear.' Mrs Margaret sigh heavy. Then she standing up, and starting make her own tea. She drink it in very thirsty way, like angry camel in the desert. I am confusing. Am I make tea for her before she asking me? But how do I know she thirsty if she not telling me directly? All this *manners* very complication. China not have *politeness* in same way.
And how to learn be *polite* if I not getting chance talk people? I am always alone, talking in my notebook, or wandering here and there like

invisible ghost. Nobody speak to me and I not dare open my mouth first because when I start talking, I asking the rude questions.

'Excuse me, you know there are some red spots on your face?'

'Are you a bit fatter than me?'

'I don't believe we same age. You look much older than me.'

'I think you are a very normal person. Not a special person.'

'The food you cook is disgusting. Why nobody tell you?'

I already have very famous reputation in my language school. They say: 'You know that Chinese girl . . . ' 'Which one?' 'That rude one of course!'. I hear it several times. Maybe I need get trained from 'Manners International Etiquette Workshop', which is advertisement I read on Chinese newspaper. It say:

Manners International custom tailors each etiquette program to the specific requirements of each individual, business/corporation, organization, school, Girl Scout Troop, or family.

I think I am exactly that 'individual' needing to be taught there, if fee is not too expensive. Re-education is always important.

Mrs Margaret look at me in sad way. 'You must be very *homesick*,' she says.

Actually not missing family at all, and not missing boring little hometown also. I happy I not needing think about stinking shoes with anyhow the same style on showroom shelfs in parent factory. I glad I not having go work every day at work unit. Only thing I missing is food. Roasted ducks, fresh cut lamb meat in boiling hot pot, and red chilli spicy fish . . . When thinking of food, I feel I make big mistake by leaving China.

This country to me, this a new world. I not having past in this country. No memory being builded here so far, no sadness or happiness so far, only information, hundreds and thousands of information, which confuse me everyday.

Except my English class every morning, I so bored of being alone. I always alone, and talking to myself. When sky become dark, I want grab something warm in this cold country. I want find friend teach me about this strange country. Maybe I want find man can love me. A man in this country save me, take me, adopt me, be my family, be my home. Every night, when I write diary, I feeling troubled. Am I writing in Chinese or in English? I trying express me, but confusing — I see other little me try expressing me in other language.

Maybe I not need feeling lonely, because I always can talk to other 'me'. Is like seeing my two pieces of lips speaking in two languages at same time. Yes, I not lonely, because I with another me. Like Austin Power with his Mini Me.

progressive tenses

(Also called 'Continuous Tenses') Progressive tenses are made with TO BE + – ING. The most common use of the progressive form is to talk about an action or situation that is already going on at a particular moment we are thinking about. But the 'going to' structure and the present progressive can also be used to talk about the future.

People say 'I'm going to go to the cinema . . . '
   Why there two *go* for one sentence? Why not enough to say one *go* to go?

> *I am going to go to the supermarket to buy some porks?*
> *You are going to go to the Oxford circus to buy clothes?*
> *He is going to go to the park for a walk?*

'I go' is enough to expressing 'I am going to go . . . ' Really.

This afternoon, I am going to go to cinema watch double bill — *Breakfast at Tiffiny's* and *Some Like it Hot*. Double bill, they letting people pay one time but twice of the bill, how clever the business here! Cinema is my paradise. When a person not having any idea about real life, just walk into cinema choosing a film to see. In China, I seeing some American films, like

39

Titanic, and *Rush Hours*, but of course Hollywood stars speaking Mandarin to us, and I can sing soundtrack from *Titanic*, 'My heart goes on and on', only in Chinese translation.

American films strange in London. People at Language School tell me use student card, I can have cheap cinema ticket. Last week I go Prince Charles in Chinatown. They say is cheapest cinema in London. Two films screening: *Moholland Driver*, and *Blue Velvet*. All together is more than 4 hours. Perfect for my lonely night. So I buy tickets and get in.

Gosh what crazy films. I not understanding very much the English speakings, but I understand I must never walk in highway at night alone. The world scary and strange like deep dark dream. Leaving cinema, trembling, I try find bus to home, but some mean kids teasing at each other on bus stop. Shouting and swearing bit like terrorist. Old man drunk in street and walk to me saying words I not understanding. Maybe he think I prostitute. England is hopeless country, but people having everything here: Queen, Buckingham Place, Loyal Family, oldest and slowest tube, BBC, Channel 4, W.H. Smith, Marx & Spencer, Tesco, Soho, millennium bridge, Tate Modern, Oxford Circus, London Tower, Cider and ale, even Chinatown.

★　★　★

Anyway, after *Breakfast at Tiffany* where posh woman dressing like prostitute and *Some Like It*

Hot where mans dressing like womans, I go back my new home which have cheap renting 65 pounds per week. It is ugly place. It smelling pee in every corner of street. Nearby tube station called Tottenham Hale.

House is two floors, lived by Cantonese family: housewife, husband who work as chef in Chinatown, and 16-year-old British-accent son. Is like one child policy still carried on here. The garden is concrete, no any green things. Very often little wild grass growing and come out between the concretes, but housewife pull and kill grass immediately. She is grass killer. The lush next doors trees trying come through rusty iron fence, but nothing getting in this concrete family. This house like factory place in China, just for cheap labours earning money, no life, no green, and no love.

Family speaks Cantonese so I not understanding them. Chinese moon calendar is on wall. Wok, chopsticks, Mah Jong, Chinese cable TV programmes . . . everything inside house is traditional. Not much fun. Outside, view is rough. Old rusty railway leading to maybe more interesting place. Walking along railway I see nearby shopping centre, a McDonalds, a KFC, a Burger King, a petrol station called 'Shell', a sad looking Tottenham Hale tube station.

Every night I coming out Tottenham Hale tube station and walking home shivering. I scared to pass each single dark corner. In this place, crazy mans or sporty kids throwing stones to you or shouting to you without reasons. Also, the robbers robbing the peoples even poorer

41

than them. In China we believe 'rob the rich to feed the poor'. But robbers here have no poetry.

'Dare to struggle and dare to win.' Chairman Mao's words like long time no see friend coming to me. I need somebody protect me, accompany me, but not staring at me in darkness. I longing for smile from man, longing for smile even only remaining several seconds.

March

homosexual

homosexual adj (person) sexually attracted to members of the same sex

I meet you in the cinema. It is film called *Fear Eats Soul*, from German director Rainer Werner Fassbinder. Programme say Fassbinder is *homosexual*. What is it? Now I have this *Collins English Dictionary* — THE AUTHORITY ON CURRENT ENGLISH. It tells me what is *Homosexual*. Strange word, I cannot imagine it.

It is the Ciné-Lumière, near South Kensington. 7 o'clock Monday, raining. Not over ten people, half are old couple with white hair. Then there you are.

You are alone. You sit almost beside me. Two seats between us. Your face quite pale in the dim light, but beautiful. I too am alone in the cinema. I always alone in the cinema before I meet you. I am bit confused whether if cinema make me less lonely or even more lonely.

On the screen, old German woman dancing with young black man in a pub. All the peoples in pub watching. Old woman she has humble smile. She has hard life. Then I see your smile in the dark light. Why I can see your smile while I am watching the film? You turn your face and understand I am looking at you. You smile again, but very gentle, and very little. You look back the screen.

You have warm smile. Is like a baby's smile. Nobody smile to me before like you in this cold country. In the darkness, I am thinking you must be kind man.

It is a film shows impossible love between old white woman and young black man. But nothing to do with 'homosexual'.

After film, we walk to exit. Our bodies so close. Out from cinema, road lights finally light up our faces.

Then, with gentle smile, you ask me:

'Did you like the film?'

I nod head.

Is like the uncomfortable English weather have some sunshine suddenly.

You ask my name. I say name start from Z, 'But please no worry to remember,' I say, 'my name too long pronounce.' You tell me your name, but how I remember English name? Western name are un-rememberable, like all Western look the same. But I want remember you, want remember the difference you with others. I look at your face. Brown eyes, transparent. Thick brown hair, like colour of leafs in autumn. Your voice gentle, but solid. It sound safe.

We walk from South Kensington towards Hyde Park. A long way for feets. What we talk about? I tell you of famous English creamy tea. You say prefer French Patisserie.

'Patty surly?'

'No *patisserie*.'

'How spell?'

'P-a-t-i-s-s-e-r-i-e.' You speak slowly with

slowly moving lips, like Mrs Margaret.

'What is it?' I not bring dictionary tonight.

You stop in front very fashionable 'French Patisserie' shop. Still open at late time. Beautiful cakes waiting inside window.

'Which one would you like?' You look at me.

I worried of price.

'I don't know,' I say. How I know about these soft stuffs?

'Then I'll choose one for you.'

You give me a piece of creamy thing.

'What is it?' I hold it on my hand carefully.

'c-h-o-c-o-l-a-t-e e-c-l-a-i-r.'

'OK.'

I bite it, but immediately cream squeeze out, falling on street.

I look at white cream drop on dirty street.

You look at white cream drop on dirty street.

'Oh well, never mind,' you say.

So we talk, and talk, and talk, through Hyde Park, then to West End, then Islington, walk towards my place. Nearly four hours walking. My legs is so sore, and my throat so dry, but I enjoying it. Is first time a person walking beside me through chilly night. Is also first time a person being patience listen my nonsense English, and learning me bad language. You much better than Mrs Margaret. She never let us talk freely.

When I arriving back, is already deep night.

In front of house, you kiss my two cheeks, and watch me go in door.

'Good meeting you,' you say.

Everything happen in very gentle way.

47

★ ★ ★

I want go immediately my room think about English man who smile and kiss me like lover, but I see Chinese landlord sitting on kitchen, watching TV and waiting for me. He is yawning. He worried my late back. At same time wife come down from upstairs bedroom in sleeping robe:

'We were so worried about you! We never come back as late as you do!'

Nervous voice remind me of my mother. My mother always talk to me like that.

I say I OK. Don't worry.

Wife look at me seriously: 'It is dangerous at night and also you are a young girl.'

I take off my guilty shoes.

'Next time if you are late, phone my husband and he can come and pick you up. This is England not China. Men easily get drunk in the pub!'

With last yawn, husband turn off TV. He look cross and tired.

I feel good after I close my bedroom's door. My heart hold a secret to make me warm at night.

The leafs blow outside. The street lights shine on my window. I am thinking I am only person to be awake in the world. I am thinking of China, thinking of old German lady dancing, thinking of your smile. I fall to sleep with sweet feelings inside my body.

guest

guest n person entertained at another's house or at another's expense; invited performer or speaker; customer at a hotel or restaurant

A new day. You call me. At once I know your voice. You ask if I want visit Kew Gardens.

'Queue Gardens?'

'Meet me at Richmond tube station,' you say. 'R-i-c-h-m-o-n-d.'

Is beautiful weather. What a surprise. And so peaceful in the grassy space. So green. Cherry blossoms is just coming out and you tell me about your favourite snowdrops. We see there is different small gardens with different theme. Africa garden are palm trees. North America garden are rocks. South America garden are cactus. And there is too Asia gardens. I so happy Manager not forgetting Asia gardens.

But I so disappointing after we walk in. Lotuses and bamboos is growing in India garden, plum trees and stone bridge is growing in Japanese garden. Where is my Chinese garden?

'Doesn't look like they've made a Chinese garden,' you say to me.

'But that very unfair,' I say in angry voice. 'Bamboos belongs to China. Panda eats

49

bamboos leafs in China, you must hear, no?'

You laugh. You say you agree. They should move some plants from India and Japan garden to make Chinese garden.

The meadow asking us to lie. We rest beside each other. I never do that with a man. Juice from grass wetting my white shirt. My heart melting. Sky is blue and airplane flying above us, low and clear. I see moving shadows of the plane on the meadow.

'I want see where you live,' I say.

You look in my eyes. 'Be my guest.'

misunderstanding

misunderstand v fail to understand properly

That's how all start. From a misunderstanding. When you say 'guest' I think you meaning I can stay in your house. A week later, I move out from Chinese landlord.

I not really have anything, only big wheel-missing suitcase. The husband helping me suitcase. The wife opening door. Your white van waiting outside, you with hands on wheel.

Husband puts wheel-missing suitcase on your van, you smile to landlord and turn engine key.

I want ask something to my landlord that I always wanting ask, so I put my head out of window:

'Why you not plant plants in your garden?'

Wife is hesitate: 'Why? It is not easy to grow plants in this country. No sun.'

For last time I look the concrete garden. Is same no story, same way as before. Like little piece of Gobi desert. What a life! Or maybe all the immigrants here living like that?

White van starting up, I respond to wife:

'Not true. Everywhere green in this country. How you say not easy growing plant here?'

We leave house behind. The couple is waving hands to me.

I say: 'Chinese strange sometimes.'

You smile: 'I don't understand you Chinese at all. But I would like to get to know you.'

We driving in high street. My suitcase lie down obediently at back. Is so easy move house like this in West? I happy I leave my grey and no fun Tottenham Hale, heading to a better area, I think. But streets becoming more and more rough. Lots of black kids shouting outside. Beggars sitting on corner with dogs, smoking, and murmuring.

'Where your house?' I ask.

'Hackney.'

'How is Hackney?'

'Hackney is Hackney,' you say.

bachelor

bachelor n unmarried man; person who holds the lowest university or college degree

Your house is old house standing lonely between ugly new buildings for poor people. Front, it lemon yellow painted. Both side of house is bricks covered by mosses and jasmine leafs. Through leafs I see house very damp and damaged. Must have lots of stories happened inside this house.

And you are really *bachelor*. Your bed is single bed. Made by several piece of big wood, with wooden boxes underneath. Old bedding sheets cover it. Must be very hard for sleep, like Chinese peasants *kang* bed. In kitchen, teacups is everywhere. Every cup different with other, big or small, half new or broken . . . So everything single, no company, no partner, no pair.

First day I arrive, our conversation like this:

I say: '*I eat. Do you eat?*'

You correct me in proper way: '*I want to eat. Would you like to eat something with me?*'

You ask: '*Would you like some coffee?*'

I say: '*I don't want coffee. I want tea.*'

You change it: '*A cup of tea would be delightful.*'

Then you laughing at my confusing face, and

you change your saying: '*I would love a cup of tea, please.*'

I ask: 'How you use word 'love' on tea?'

* * *

First time you make food for me it is some raw leafs with two boiled eggs. Eggy Salad. Is that all? Is that what English people offer in their homes? In China, cold food for *guest* is bad, only beggars no complain cold food. Maybe you don't know how cook, because you are a *bachelor*.

I sit down on your kitchen table, eat silently. Lampshade is on top of my head, tap is dripping in sink. So quiet. Scarily. I never ate such a quiet food in China. Always with many of family members, everybody shouting and screaming while eating. Here only the noise is from me using the forks and knife. I drop the knife two times so I decide only use one fork in my right hand.

Chewing. Chewing. No conversation.

You look at me eating, patiently.

Finally you ask: '*So, do you like the food?*'

I nod, put another leaf into my mouth. I remember me is bad speak with food full of my mouth. You wait. But patience maybe running out, so you answer your question in my voice: '*Yes, I like the food very much. It is delicious. It is yami.*'

The memory becomes so uncertain.

The memory keeps a portrait about you. An abstract portrait like pictures I saw in Tate Modern, blur details and sketchy lines. I start draw this picture, but my memory about you keep changing, and I have to change the picture.

green fingers

green fingers *Brit. Informal* skill in gardening

Our first night. First time we make love. First time in my life doing this.

I think you are beautiful. You are beautiful smiles, and beautiful face, and beautiful language. You speak slowly. I almost hear every single word because you speak so slowly, only sometime I not understanding what you mean. But I understanding you more than anybody else I meet in England.

Then you are taking off clothes.

I look at you. Man's body seems ugly. Hair, bones, muscles, skins, more hair. I smell at you. Strong smell. Smell animal. Smell is from your hair, your chest, your neck, your armpit, your skin, your every single little bit in body.

Strong smell and strong soul. I even can feel it and touch it. And I think your body maybe beautiful also. Is the home of your soul.

I ask how old are you, is first question Chinese people ask to stranger. You say forty-four. Older than me twenty years. Forty-four in my Chinese think is old, is really old. Leaves far behind away from youth. I say age sound old, but you look young. You say thanks, and you don't say more.

I say I think you beautiful, ignoring the age. I

think you too beautiful for me, and I don't deserve of you.

* * *

Very early morning. You are sleeping, with gentle breathe. I look through bedroom's window. Sky turning dim into bright. I see small dried up old grapes hang under vines by window. Their shapes are become clear and clear in cold spring morning light. Garden is messy and lush. Your clothes and socks hanging in washing line. Your gardening machines everywhere on soil.

You are man, handy and physical. This is man's garden.

You make me feel fragile. Love makes me feel fragile, because I am not beautiful, I never being told I am beautiful. My mother always telling me I am ugly. 'You are ugly peasant girl. You have to know this.' Mother tells this to me for all twenty-three years. Maybe why I not never having boyfriend like other Chinese girls my age. When I badly communicating with others, my mother's words becomes loud in my eardrum. I am ugly peasant girl. I am ugly peasant girl.

'My body is crying for you,' you say.

Most beautiful sentence I heard in my life.

My bad English don't match your beautiful language.

I think I fall in love with you, but my love cannot match your beauty.

* * *

57

And then daytime. Sun puts light through garden to our bed. Birds are singing on roof. I think how sunlight must make people much happier in this dark country and then I watch you wake up. We see each other naked, without distance. In light of reality. 'Good morning,' you say. 'You look even more lovely than yesterday.' And we make love again in the morning.

fertilise

fertilise v provide (an animal or plant) with sperm or pollen to bring about fertilisation; supply (soil) with nutrients

You take me to garden. Is very small, maybe ten square metres. One by one, you introduce me all the plants you have put there. Sixteen different plants in a ten square metres garden. In my home town in China, there only one plant in fields: rice.

You know every single plant's name, like they your family and you try tell me but I not remember English names so you write them down:

Potato	Green beans
Daffodil	Wisteria
Lavender	Grape vine
Mint	Bay tree
Spinach	Geranium
Thyme	Beetroot
Dill	Sweet corn
Apple tree	Fig tree

Then I tell you all these plants have very different names and meanings in Chinese. So I write down names in Chinese, and explain every word at you.

59

Potato 土豆

earth bean

Daffodil 水仙

fairy maiden from the water

Lavender 熏衣草

clothes perfuming weeds

Mint 薄荷

light lotus

Spinach 菠菜

watery vegetable

Thyme 百里香

one hundred miles fragrant

Dill 莳萝

the herb of time

Apple tree 苹果树

clover fern fruit tree

Green beans 豆子

son of beans

Wisteria 紫藤

purple vines

| Grape vine | 葡萄 |
| | crawling plant |

| Bay tree | 月桂树 |
| | moon laurel |

| Geranium | 天竺葵 |
| | sky bamboo flower |

| Beetroot | 甜菜 |
| | sweet vegetable |

| Sweet corn | 玉米 |
| | jade rice |

| Fig tree | 无花果树 |
| | the fruit tree without flowers |

You laughing when you hear the names. 'I never knew flutes grew on trees,' you say. It seems I am big comedy to you. I not understand why so funny. 'You can't say your Rs. It's *fruit* not *flute*,' you explain me. 'A *flute* is a musical instrument. But your Chinese name seems just right: a fig tree really is a fruit tree without flowers.'

'How a tree can just have fruit without having flower first?' I ask.

Like teacher, you describe how insect climbs into fruit to fertilise seed.

What 'fertilise'? I need looking in *Concise Chinese-English Dictionary*.

'Fertilise' make me think Chairman Mao. He likes fertiliser. Was big Mao thing increase productivity, increase plants. Maybe that why China, biggest peasants population country, still alive and become stronger after using fertiliser on the soil.

I ask: 'How long a fig tree has figs after insects fertilising it? Like woman have ten months pregnant?'

You look at me, like look at *alien*.

'Why ten months? I thought it took nine months,' you say.

'Chinese we say *shi yue huai tai* (十月怀胎). It means giving the birth after ten months pregnant.'

'That's strange.' You seem like want to laugh again. 'Which day do you start to count the pregnancy in China?' you ask seriously. But how I know? We never being taught this *properly* in school. Too shameful to teach and to study for our Chinese.

Standing under your fruit tree without flowers, I pick up piece of leaf, and put on my palm. A single leaf, but large. I touch the surface and feel hairy.

'Have you read the Bible?' you ask.

'No.' Of course not, not in China.

You fetch a big huge black book from room. You open the pages. 'Actually the fig tree is the oldest of mankind's symbols.' You point at beginning of book:

And the eyes of them both were opened, and they knew that they were naked, and they sewed fig leaves together, and made themselves aprons.

'What is that?' I am curious.

'It is about Adam and Eve. They used fig leaves to cover their naked bodies.'

'They clever. They knowing fig leaves bigger than other leafs,' I say.

You laugh again.

Your gardening machines everywhere in disorder.

Spade 铲子

For cutting the soil

Fork 叉子

For soften the soil

Rake 耙子

For scratching the grass

Suddenly I bit shocked, stop. There are some nudity in your garden.

'What this?' I ask.

'Those are my sculptures,' you say.

Sculptures? A naked man no head, facing to ground of the garden. Body twisted, with enormous hands and enormous feet. Close to ground, between the legs, two beautiful eggs, like two half of apples. In the middle of apples, a penis like little wounded bird. I walk to him and

63

touch. Is made of plaster. I amazed by this body, is huge, looks suffered. I remember picture from Michelangelo's *David* on your bookshelf, a very healthy and balanced body. But yours, yours far different.

Beside this body statue, some other smalls clay sculptures. Ear, big like basin, in brown. Shape of that ear spread like a big flower. Then more ears, different shape, different size. They lie on the grass quietly, listening us.

Under fig tree another penis made from clay, gentle, innocent. Then another one, looks harder, lies down beside honeysuckle roots, in soil colour. Little clay sculptures there, like they live with plants hundred years.

The noisy London being stopped by brick wall. The grey city kept away by this garden. Plants and sculptures on sunshine. Glamorous, like you. Maybe all mans in London green fingers. Maybe this country too cold and too dim, so plants and garden can showing imagination the spring, the sun, the warmth. And plants and garden giving love like womans warm mans life.

When I stand in garden with sixteen different plants, I think of Chinese mans. Chinese city-mans not plant-lover at all. Shameful for Chinese city-mans pour passion onto those leafs. He be considered a loser, no position in society. But you, you different. Who are you?

instruction

instruction n order to do something; teaching pl information on how to do or use something

We have so much sex. We make love every day and every night. Morning, noon, afternoon, late afternoon, evening, early night, late night, midnight, even in the dreams. We make love in sun, we make love in grey afternoon, and we make love at raining night. We make love on narrow bench of garden, under fig tree, on hammock covered by the grape leafs, by kitchen sink, on dinner table, on anywhere we feel like to make love. I feel scared towards your huge energy. You come into me strong like a storm blowing a wooden house in the forest, and you come into me deep like a hammer beating the nail on the wall. You ask me if it feels good, and I say it make me feel comfortable.

'Only *comfortable*!?'

'Yes,' I tell you. 'I find your body is very comfortable, like nothing else I find in this uncomfortable country.'

Do I feel shame about sex? Yes, I do, in beginning. A lot. Is such taboo in China. I never really know what is sex before. Now I naked everyday in the house, and I can see clearly my desire. Recent I dream few times that I am naked

65

in street, in market, and even on highway. I run through busy street fast as I can to get home. But still, everybody in street surprising to see I am naked.

What this dream about?

You say this dream about shame or fear of being exposed.

Every time we make love you produce so much sperm on my skin like the spring on the Trafagar Square, you are worried sometimes that maybe I get pregnant. We only want have each other and we don't want let the third person take over our love.

You say we need use the condom.

In our long-shabby-Hackney-Road, there no any '*Boots*' (*Boots* is a shop represent civilisation to me), although *Cost Cutter* sells condom sometimes. But shopkeeper in *Cost Cutter* know us just like he know niece or nephew. And he is serious Muslim, he might anti condom user. So we have go to Brick Lane, where the Bangladeshi shopkeepers are kind and messy, and they can't remembering every single customer face whom from Hackney Road.

★ ★ ★

PLEASE READ THESE INSTRUCTIONS CARE-FULLY, as it say on the box. I open box, unfold notes, then start read. I never read condom instruction before. I think people maybe only read condom instruction when the first time they try to sex. Anyway I new to this.

Tear along one side of the foil, removing

the condom carefully. Condoms are strong but can be torn by sharp fingernails or jewellery.

'What is *jewellery?*' I ask.

'Sparkly stuff women love to wear,' you say, without emotion.

Only put the condom on when the penis is erect and before contact with your partner's body. This helps prevent STDs and pregnancy.

'What is *STD?*'

'Sexually Transmitted Disease,' you reply quickly, as if is thing you are familiar as your every day's mint tea.

Now place the condom over the end of the penis with the roll on the outside. With one hand pinch the teat of the condom to expel any trapped air, this will make space for the sperm.

I being stopped by these word: **one hand pinch the teat of the condom to expel any trapped air . . . I** needing several seconds to imagine that scene. Is like pornography. We cannot have words like this in Chinese. We too ashamed. Westerner has nothing too ashamed. You can do anything in this country.

Using the other hand, roll the condom down the length of the penis to its base. Withdraw the penis soon after ejaculation whilst still erect, holding the condom firmly in place at the base of the penis. Wait until the penis is completely withdrawn before removing the condom. Keep the penis and condom away from the vagina to avoid any

67

contact with sperm . . .

I can't continuing reading. I am totally lost these words. But you laughing.

Condoms are intended for vaginal intercourse, other uses can increase the potential for breakage.

I stop: 'What's that mean?'

'It is a hint. It means you shouldn't put it into the arse.' You answer, very precise, but no more patience, as you start reading your *Guardian Weekend*.

I read other bits of instruction on other side as well, and they less important. For example,

Even if you are not planning on having sexual intercourse, it's sensible to carry condoms with you, just in case.

Sensible to carry condoms all the time? Westerner can always have sex whenever they go shopping, or waiting for bus or train. Sex in this country is like brush the hair or the teeth.

Words on the instruction are more exciting than sexy magazines on shelfs of corner shop in our street.

charm

charm n attractive quality; trinket worn on a bracelet; magic spell v attract, delight; influence by personal charm; protect or influence as if by magic

From first day we being together, until next two and three days, our skins being non stop together, not separating even a hour. You talk to me about everything. But I not understand completely. You say:

'I used to try to love men. For most of the last twenty years I have been out with men.'
I think is good try love men. World better place. But go out where?

'When I was a squatter, I made a lot of sculptures. They'd fill the houses.'
What *squat*? I take out dictionary. Says 'to sit with the knees bent and the heels close to the bottom or thighs.' Very difficult position, I imagine.
What kind houses you squatted there? Don't lonely sit with the knees bent without chair on the floor?

'I used to plant potatoes and beans on a farm, and I looked after my goats. I loved doing that, more than anything else.'

So you a peasant? How come you also such a city man?

'I love old things. I love second-hand things. I hate new things. I don't want to buy new things any more.'

But old things rotten, dying. How you feel alively and active with daily life if only live with old things?

★ ★ ★

Every sentence you said, I put into my own dictionary. Next day I look at and think every single word. I am entering into your brain. Although my world so far away from your, I think I be able understand you. I think you absolutely *charming*. Thing around you fascinating.

I feel a concentrate of love for you, farmer, sculptor, lover of men, stranger. Noble man.

In China we say hundreds of reincarnations bring two peoples to same boat. Maybe you are that people for me to be same boat. I never met mans like you before. I think we perfect: You quite Yin, and I very Yang. You earthy, and I metal. You bit damp, and I a little dry. You cool, and I hot. You windy, and I firey. We join. There is mutualism. And we can benefit each other. And all these makes us efficient lover.

vegetarian

vegetarian n person who eats no meat or fish
adj suitable for a vegetarian

One problem between us and that is food.

Chop Chop, local Chinese restaurant in
Hackney. I make you go there even though you
say you never go Chinese restaurants.

Restaurant has very plain looking. White
plastic table and plastic chairs and white
fluorescent lamp. Just like normal government
work unit in China. Waiter unhappy when
cleans table, not looking anybody. Woman
with pony tails behind counter she even more
mean. A plastic panda-savings-tin sitting on
top of counter. None of them can speak
Mandarin.

'No. Sit there. No, no, not this table. Sit at that
table.'

Waiter commands like we is his soldiers.

'What you want? . . . We don't have tap
water, you have to order something from the
menu . . . We don't do pots of green tea, only
cups.'

I hate them. I swear I never been so rude
Chinese restaurant in my entirely life. Why
Chinese people becoming so mean in the West?
I feel bit guilty for horrible service. Because I

bring you, and you maybe thinking my culture just like this. Maybe that why some English look down of our Chinese. I am shameful for being a Chinese here.

But we still have to eat. Especially me, starving like the Ghost of Hunger. I always hungry. Even after big meal, later by one or two hours I feel hungry again. My family always very poor until several years ago. We used eat very small, barely had meat. After my parents started shoes factory, and left the poor peasants background behind, changed. But still I think foods all the time.

You not know nothing about Chinese food so I quickly order: duck, pork, fried tofu with beefs.

Meal comes to table, and I digging fastly my chopsticks into dishes like having a snowstorm. But you don't have any action at all. You just look me, like looking a Beijing opera.

'Why you not eat?' I ask, busy chewing my pork in my mouth.

'I am not very hungry,' you say.

'You use chopsticks?' I think maybe that's the reason.

'Yes. Don't worry.' You raise your chopsticks and perform to me.

'But you waste the food. Not like Chinese food?'

'I am a *vegetarian*,' you say picking up little bit rice. 'This menu is a zoo.'

I am surprised. I try find my dictionary. Damn, is not with me this time. I remember film *English Patient* I watch on pirate DVD in

China to education me about British people. 'What that word? Word describe a people fall asleep for long long time, like living dying?'

'You mean coma?' You are confused.

'Yes, that is the word! You are not like that, do you?'

You put chopsticks down. Maybe you angry now.

'I presume you are thinking of the *persistent vegetative state*,' you say. '*Vegetarian* means you don't eat meat.'

'Oh, I am sorry,' I say, swallowing big mouthful tofus and beefs.

Now I understand why never buy piece of meat. I thought it is because you poor.

'Why don't eat meat? Meat very nutritious.'

' . . . ' You have no comments.

'Also you be depression if you don't eating meat.'

' . . . ' You still have no comments.

'My parents beaten me if I don't eating meat or any food on table in a meal. My parents curse me being picky and spoiled. Because others dying without any food to eat.'

' . . . ' Still don't say anything.

'How come man is vegetarian? Unless he is monk,' I say.

Still no words from you, but laughing.

You watch me eating all of meal. I try finish the duck, and the tofu and the beefs. My stomach painful. There are still porks left, and I order to take them away.

While I eating, you write top ten favorite food on a napkin:

lettuce

carrot

lentils

broccoli

radish

aubergine

avocado

pumpkin

spinach

asparagus

But, is this list will be the menu in our kitchen for rest of life? Is terrible! What about my meatball, my mutton, my beefs in black bean sauce? Who will be in charge of kitchen?

noble

noble adj showing or having high moral qualities; of the nobility; impressive and magnificent

Sunday. I want do shopping. I say we need buy some toilet paper, some candle, some garlic, some ginger, some greens. (I not say meat, but actually that what I want buy after eating vegetables with you every day.)

'I want go to Sainsbury.' After saying that, I realising I need practise my English manner, so I ask you again: 'Shall we go to Sainsbury?'

You not look happy.

'Hmm, right. Let's worship in Sainsbury's every Sunday.'

'What worship?'

'Worship? It's how the Chinese feel about Mao.'

I don't know what say. Don't you know now we worship America?

'I don't like Sainsbury's,' you say. 'I like the rubbish market. They have much more interesting things there.'

'Which rubbish market?'

You take me to the Brick Lane market. Is really a rubbish market. All kind of second-hand or third-hand radios, old CDs, used furniture, broken television set (who want buy a broken TV set?), old bicycles, tyres, nails, drilling machines, dusty shoes, pirate DVDs, cheap biscakes . . . I wonder if all these things made in China.

You walk in the rubbish market with your old brown leather jacket and your dirty old leather shoes. The jacket is so old that the sleeves are wore out and the bottom is pieces. But you look great with these rubbish costumes in the rubbish market.

★　★　★

I think you are a *noble* man with *noble* words. I am not noble. I am humble. And I speak humble English. I from poor town in south China. We never see noble.

April

surprise

surprise n unexpected event; amazement and wonder v cause to feel amazement or wonder; come upon, attack, or catch suddenly and unexpectedly

Suddenly another thing else new and unexpected:

'I need to leave London for a few days.' You pack clothes.

'For what? For where?' It is too out in blue for me.

'To see my friend Jack, in Devon.'

'Who is Jack? I never heard you talk about him.'

'Well, I have lots of friends.'

'I come with you.' I starting open wardrobe to take some clothes out.

'No. You don't have to.'

'I want to.'

'No, I'm going on my own.'

'Why?'

'I just don't think it's the right time for you to come.'

'Why not?'

'Well, I have my own life . . . '

I don't understand you mean: 'But we go together. We lovers!'

I upset. Your decision destroying image of perfectness.

'Come next time,' you say.

I stop. Don't know what do.

'How many days away? I will feel lonely.'

'Just three or four.'

I can't say anything. But what I am do without you here in house? I even don't knowing where electricity box, and how answer telephone in proper way.

'You know, you've got to go out and make some friends,' you say, 'so you're not always dependent on me. What about those girls from your language school?'

'Don't need another friends. I don't want. I only want be with you.'

You pack some your stuffs. You walk to the back room. Five seconds, you pushing blue bicycle out.

'This is for you. I bought it in Brick Lane. Look, you can wear a skirt — there's no bar in between.'

'Try it,' you say.

I don't care the bicycle. I walk and hug you tightly. I put my head into your old leather jacket.

Finally, you leave. White van stays outside. You take bus and then you will take train. England is small country compare China, but still, I feel you leaving me somewhere far away, somewhere unknown, somewhere I don't involve at all.

I thought we together, we will spend time together and our lifes will never separated. I thought I don't needing go these double-bill screenings to kill raining nights. I thought I will not scared to live in this country alone, because now I having you, and you my family, my home. But I wrong. You doesn't promise anything solid.

So now I go out into the world on my alone . . . with that blue bicycle. And remind me to ride on left side at all times.

pub

pub n building with a bar licensed to sell alcoholic drinks

Park my bicycle outside from Dirty Dick's, nearby Liverpool Street Station. Dirty Dick? That normal name for English pub? Anyway, it is first time I came into *building with a bar licensed to sell alcoholic drinks*. I hope you will take me into pub, but you went away somewhere unknown instead.

I sit in pub alone, trying feel involving in the conversation. It seem place of middle-aged-mans culture. I smell a kind of dying, although it still struggling. While I sitting here, many singles, desperately mans coming up saying, 'Hello darling'. But I not your darling. Where your darling? 7 o'clock in the evening, your darling must be cooking baked bean in orange sauce for you at home . . . Why not just go home spending time with your darling?

But mans here just keep buying pint of beer one after another. Some is drinking huge pint Lager, is like pee. Others buying glass of very dark liquid, looks like Chinese medicine. They watching football and shout together, without having food. In corner some tables with foods. Make me feel very hungry. See the food is biggest reason I am deciding go to pub. But everyone pretending food not there. Like is invisible or just for the good show. I take out my *Concise Chinese-English Dictionary*, start to study. I trying not thinking of the food too much.

In front of my table, five big mans all smoking cigarettes; this is the *fog* of London. After some times, mans come to my lonely table and ask something.

The way I am talking in English make everybody laugh. They must like me.

A young man buy me beer. He is the only good looking one.

I say: 'I feel so delightful drinking with you. Your face and words are very *noble*.'

The man surprised and happy. He stops his drinking.

'Noble, eh?'

'Yes,' I say, 'because when you start talk then you look very proud. I like the confidence. I don't have.'

The man holding his big pint listens careful but not sure about what I mean.

A while, he says: 'Love, you only think my words are noble because I can speak English properly' — oh *properly*, that word again! — 'but it *is* my mother tongue, you know. It's not that hard. But anyway, thank you for the compliment.'

'You deserving it.' I answer seriously.

But the man calls me 'Love'! Love is cheap object in London.

My eyes looking towards delicious feast on

side table. Everything ready waiting but no action.

I think the man gets hint from me, so he introduces me to English food system in pub calling *Buffet*, is meaning same word for 'self service'.

'Why two words for same food system?' I ask him.

He laughs: 'Because one is the English word and one is the French word. The French word is more *noble*.'

All old mans laughing.

Buffet. Now I remember this noble word.

There are some white sticky stuffs on the plate. It looks like Tofu, but smells bad.

'What is this?' I ask bar man.

'That is goat's cheese, darling. Would you like to try some?'

In China we not have cheese. We not like drinking milk, until last ten years maybe. I feel very surprise. I thought goat is too skinny make cheese.

'No. Thanks. What that? That Blue stuff?'

'It's another cheese. Stilton.'

'Another stinking cheese with different names?' So many different cheeses! Like our Tofu system!

'Is this made by cow?' I ask.

'That's right, love,' the barman laughs loudly. 'Handmade by Communist cows.'

'What?' I am confused.

'Sorry to tease you, sweetheart. What you're trying to ask is 'Is it made *from* cow's milk?' English is a bloody nightmare, isn't it?'

Back home I write list my new learnings for Mrs Margaret: *made by, made from*.

drifter

drifter n person who moves aimlessly from place to place or job to job; a fishing boat equipped with drift nets

Third day you are away. Feels like you are gone for a month. Before, I never be alone living in this house. Now, I realise this *your* house. Everything yours, and everything in this place *made by* you. Very little to do with me. But this place completely take over my life. I am a little alone teacup belonging to your cupboard.

I wandering in your house, silently, lonely, like cat without master.

On your dusty books shelf, I take out photo album.

There is picture of you, arms around big tree, like lover. You naked in the picture. Very young and with a brown skin. You smiling at the person with camera. Must be your lover.

Another picture, you on boat. Is old black and white photo, so sea looks totally brown. You only wear shorts, and your muscles are strong. You smile to camera, holding the boat's paddle.

Who with you on that boat? Which sea it is?

Another old picture, you are with a man, a

85

young man. You both are naked, standing on rock by the sea. The waves coming up on your legs. Man beside you is handsome. Who is person taking this photo? Man or woman? You must be three very intimate, very close friend, if you both naked in front the camera.

Putting back photo album, I am jealous, and I feel the pain from my jealousy.

I open one of your old boxes on top the books shelf. Some letters inside. I think they are love letters. Letters you wrote and being returned from somebody in a one big package. You said in one letter:

> Of course I am ~~about~~ committed to you, and I always will be. But I can never see myself in a couple. Yes, you are my lover, but you are also my friend, and we will always feel special together. Friendship always ~~lasts~~ endures longer than romance.

Romance not to be found in my *Concise Chinese-English Dictionary*.

Some your old diaries in box too, from 1970s and 1980s. A long time ago. When I was really little. Gosh, this is the man really older than me twenty years. Twenty years of extra life. You from such a different world.

Something is very important about this word *drifter*. I meet it in your letters, or the letters somebody wrote to you, or in diary with broken pages; I meet it everywhere in your long-ago past, but I never understand what it mean.

I have to learning this word first, then to learning something about you.

Open your old *Roget's Thesaurus* on your shelf (*Thesaurus*! More strange word! In Chinese, we not having a second word to replace 'dictionary'!) On the cover: *first published 1852*. Gosh! 1852. That an old dictionary. In China there is very old Character Dictionary from 1700s Kang Xi era but I only know not half of the characters.

Thesaurus only make me more confusing. Drifter like fishing boat? Drifter goes fishing on a fishing boat? Or situation of a fishing boat swing in the sea is like situation of drifter?

I think of that picture you are on the boat wearing the shorts, holding the paddle, smiling the camera. Behind you is brown colour sea. You a drifter, I believe.

In your diary, you describing your father a drifter. He is bus driver, and he doesn't like stay at home. Don't know why. One day he leave you and mother and sisters and never came back. You say you learned your father travels anywhere hot and anywhere can have sex. Gosh, I can't believe what I read. Your mother decide buy piece of farm in Cornwall. Farm has a name called Lower End Farm. She live with sheep and goats and cows. Without any mans around.

You grow up, feeling cold from your family. You feel womans so dull and womans not

87

interesting. You wanting something exciting and something desirable. So you decide leave find a place far away from that cold farm, a place cannot reach your mother and your tough sisters. You love the sea and you want see the world.

When nineteen you go to long voyage with man from your hometown. From your diary, I think he called John. Boat belonging to John's. You young and you write diary because you think that is your historic time in life.

The first page of your sailing diary:

February 6th 1978
We are all looking forward to sailing but at the moment we're blinded by the work and preparation needed before we set out. Yesterday I nearly I think it's going to be a really exciting trip during which much will be learnt by everyone.

At the end of that day, underneath the page, you wrote a line in capital:

'ROMANTIC IRELAND'S DEAD AND GONE' - W.B. YEATS

Another page, words is soaked by water. Difficult read:

Sunday 11ᵗʰ February

We have eventually left amidst cheers from our friends on the quayside... We were all pleased to get away from what was beginning to become a stale atmosphere where no one could do anything without consulting someone else. I couldn't At first I felt pure excitement, but later when the open sea was below us, I started feeling sick. Our watch began

The writing start becoming very messy and un-readable.

I open last page on diary and find out you spend nine months on boat all together. From February 1978 to 4 November 1978. How a person can do for so long without his feet stand on soil? I imagine you must be suffered from storms. Sometimes you must be burning by sun. Were you ill on boat in all nine months? Did you wish you be anywhere but not on boat?

You saying in your journey sometimes you feel life exciting because you are on enormous sea, sailing and sailing for ever, but sometime you really bored in every single minute because you are always on boundless sea, sailing and sailing for ever. I try imagine to watch sea every single minute but can't. I never even been close sea. Only watched from plane.

89

June 7ᵗʰ 1978

Breakfast: tuna. Supper: tuna, I try to eat as much green veg as I can, but the fridge is well guarded (a tomato went missing yesterday)

Panama, Costa Rica, Nicaragua, El Salvador, Guatemala. These are the central American countries which we have passed, although some we have not seen because the boat has been too far out to sea.

Next page, you arrive San Diego and San Francisco.

You not really write about love. Was love not in your nineteen-year-old life? Is really only blue sea in your brown eyes at that time? What about your dreams?

⋆　⋆　⋆

After that long voyage, you longing for something you can do with your hands. Twenty years old, you go art school. You studying sculptures there by making your hands dirty. A photo between the pages. I guess was that the sculpture you made. Enormous naked man, lying down and taking over whole floor of big studio. A giant, but naked giant. That the main subject of your sculptures. Then you writing you have

90

sex with several boys in that art school.

First I think I reading wrong and you mean girls not boys, but then I look again. Matt, Dan, Peter. These are boys names.

'*I don't feel any real love in my heart*,' you write.

When you move London, you go *squat* in old houses and meet mans in street every night. You talk to the strangers in the park and you go to home together. You say you feel warm by touching other's body, by having sex with mans. You think you a homosexual, you call it *Gay*. But you even can't remember faces and names the second day.

Then there is another diary. Is some years later. You feel empty that kind of hunting-boy-life, so you become campaigner, a demonstrator. You for campaign against the capitalism, against the McDonald developing, and you go India stopping mining companies doing developmenting there. You go with young demon-strater group to everywhere, Delhi, Calcutta, Mexico, Los Angeles ... Always drifting around. But I thinking maybe you not know what want to do in your life. Or why you travel so much? In those *squatter*'s days, the sculpture you made are all destroyed. Nothing left. You don't have a woman lover being with you (or maybe you never want to?), and you don't have a man lover being with you either. Only thing you had, you wrote, is '*sex and seduction*'.

You wrote about days you work as youth worker. I didn't understand what this job about.

91

You wrote about holiday trips with children. There photos between pages: you with teenagers laughing in front of camera. You love those teenage boys. You work that for ten years. But how come you stop a job which you really like? I don't understand. Maybe because your *gay* life? Maybe kind of scandal as homosexual teacher. I never know . . . Anyway you left your job, and what happening next?

★   ★   ★

My eyes becoming sore. I am tired of reading, all these words, my brain is just too full by your past. Everywhere is you, and you are everywhere, every sentence, every page.

I put back all these old diaries, old letters. My hand covered by dust. I wash my hand, under cold tap water. I thinking probably you never read these things for long time. Maybe I am first person opening these boxes in last twenty years.

Night is long. Quiet outside. Cars passing sometimes. I sit on your chair. I feel bit heavy. I feel bit difficult to breathe.

I sleep on your bed alone, which we slept every night together since I move in. Actually is single bed supposed be for one person. I realise this again. I am awake. I trying draw map of you, map of your past. But is difficult. I see the morning lights outside through the garden, through fruit tree without flowers. Is fourth day you away and is the day you will be return. You said you be here in the morning, about half past ten.

Nine o'clock now. I get up, and I brush my teeth, and I make some tea. I put my cold hand on teapot to get warm. I wait for you to return. But now I scared about you to return. You will drift with your Chinese woman, in boat on the ocean. No seashore in distance. She floating away and passing in your life like piece of wood on the sea.

One hour going by, and waiting is painful. I try study *singular* and *plural* from textbook which Mrs Margaret give to us.

child — children   ox — oxen
mouse — mice   fairy — fairies
tooth — teeth   thief — thieves
goose — geese   foot — feet
wolf — wolves   larva — larvae

I don't like plural, because they not stable. I don't like nouns too, as they change all the time like verbs. I like only adjectives, and adverbs. They don't change. If I can, I will only speak adjectives and adverbs.

A quarter past eleven, you come back with a cold wind through door. You put down dusty bag on floor then you kiss me, you hug me. You are pleased to see me. I ask how is your friend, you say everything is fine. You smile and you are excited and you want make love. Like nothing happened. You say you miss me. But how I can miss someone easy coming easy going?

'Did you have a nice time?' you ask.

'No.'

'Why not? Did you go out to see people and make friends?'

'No. I don't want make friends.'

'So what did you do?'

What to say? I feel the sea inside me too big, too never-ending to speak.

bisexual

bisexual adj sexually attracted to both men and women

I am a woman and you are a bisexual. Both love beautiful mans so much. But beautiful young mans is always living in our imagination. He is daily life's fantasy. The reality about him so fragile that is easy to be broken, like delicate Chinese vase.

You have so many books to do with naked mans. On your shelf: *The Nude Male, Gay Writing From India, The Penguin Book Of International Gay Writing, Fully Exposed — the Male Nude in Photography* . . . How I know you not going to go with the beautiful gay man again and ruin my life? How I trust you stay with me? Maybe I ruin rest of my life to be with you.

Is there lots of free love in gay's world because they not produce children? No children then no serious weight. They not need considering responsibilities of next generation, and they not need worry about the pregnancy/abortion. But how that work if far-east foreign woman fall in love with West gay man?

When we see beautiful mans in street, or when we talk to beautiful mans in pub, we have very different view. You always wondering how he will look like when naked, just like you look at good painting carefully with magnifying glass. But my first question to that man more practical: will he possible become my husband? If so, will he having stable incomes and be able buy house for his family?

chinese cabbage + english slug

cabbage n vegetable with a large head of green leaves

slug n land snail with no shell; a bullet; a mouthful of an alcoholic

Hardly days is absolutely sunny, sunny until sun falling to the west. Sky in England always look suspicious, untrustful, like today's. You see me sad but don't understand why.

Standing in the garden, you ask me: 'Do you want to have your own little plants in this garden? I think it should be a woman's garden as well.'

'Yes. I want. I want plant Chinese cabbages, some water lily, some plum tree, and maybe some bamboos, and maybe some Chinese chives as well . . .'

I immediately image picture of tradition Chinese garden.

'No, honey, it's too small for so many Chinese plants.'

Then, Sunday, we went to Columbia Road Flower Market. It my favourite market. We brought the small little sprouts of Chinese cabbage at home. Eight little sprouts all together.

We plant all these little things. Digging the

soil, and putting every single sprout into the hole. You are fast than me. So you finished planting five, and I only putting third one in the little hole.

We watering Chinese cabbage sprouts every morning, loyal and faithful, like every morning we never forgetting brushing our teeth. Seeing tiny sprouts come out, my heart feel happy. Is our love. We plant it.

You say:

'Growing a vegetable and seeing it grow is more interesting than anything else. It's magic. Don't you agree?'

Yes. Is interesting. But in China, is just for peasant. Every person can do this, nothing special for growing food. Why so different here?

Then we see some little leafs come out but are bitten by the slug.

'It's dangerous that the slugs keep eating the small sprouts. They can die really easily,' you tell me.

Carrying with torch, every night, around 11 o'clock, you sneek into garden and check the slug. They are always several slug hidden behind the young leafs. Enjoying the delicious meal under the moonlight. You taking them out from the leafs, one by one. You putting these slug together in one glass bottle. Soon glass bottle becomes a slug-zoo.

★   ★   ★

'What your favourite words? Give me ten,' I say when we are sitting in garden. I want learn most

98

beautiful English words because you are beautiful. I even not care whether if useful.

A piece of blank paper, a pen.

You writing it down, one by one.

'*Sea, breath, sun, body, seeds, bumble bee, insects.*' You stop: 'How many are there now?'

'Seven,' I say.

'Hm . . . *blood* . . . ' you continue.

'Why you like blood?'

'I don't know. I feel blood is beautiful.'

'Really? But blood violence, and pain.'

'No. Not always. Blood gives you life. It makes you strong.' You speaking with surely voice.

You see things from such different perspective from me. I wonder if we change perspective one day.

'And why *breath*, then?'

'Because that's where everything is from and how everything starts.'

You are right.

'So, what else? Last favourite word?' I say.

'Suddenly.'

'*Suddenly*! Why you like *suddenly*? *Suddenly* not even noun.' You a strange brain, I think.

'Well, I just like it,' you say. 'So what are your favorite ten words?'

I write down one by one:

'*Fear, belief, heart, root, challenge, fight, peace, misery, future, solitude* . . . '

'Why *solitude*?'

'Because a song from Louis Armstrong calling 'Solitude'. It is so beautiful.' I hear song in my ear now.

'Where did you hear that song?' you ask.

'On your shelfs. A CD, from Louis Arm-strong.'

'Really? I didn't even know I had that CD.' You frown.

'Yes, is covering the dust, and look very old.'

'So, you've been through all my CDs?'

'Of course,' I say. 'I read your letters and diaries as well.'

'What?'

'And looked your photo.'

'What? You've looked through all my stuff?' You seeming like *suddenly* hear the alien from Mars attack the Earth.

'Not all. Parts that diary are make me sad. I can't sleep at night,' I say.

privacy

privacy n the state of being alone or undisturbed; freedom from interference or public attention

'You've invaded my privacy! You can't do that!' First time, you shout to me, like a lion.

'What privacy? But we living together! No privacy if we are lovers!'

'Of course there is! Everybody has privacy!'

But why people need privacy? Why privacy is important? In China, every family live together, grand-parents, parents, daughter, son, and their relatives too. Eat together and share everything, talk about everything. Privacy make people lonely. Privacy make family fallen apart.

When I arguing about privacy, you just listen and not say anything. I know you disagree me, and you not want live inside of my life, because you a 'private' person. A private person doesn't share life.

'When I read your past, when I read those letters you wrote, I think you are *drifter*.'

'What do you mean by that?'

'You know what is drifter, do you? You come and leave, you not care about future.'

'To me, to live life is to live in the present.'

'OK, live in present, and which direction you leading then?'

'What are you talking about?'

'I mean, you don't have plan for tomorrow, for next year?'

'Well, we are talking about different things. I don't think you understand what I am saying. To me the future is about moving on, to some new place. I don't know where I am going. It's like I am riding a horse through the desert, and the horse just carries me somewhere, maybe with an oasis, but I don't know.'

Suddenly the air being frozen. Feeling cold. I not know what to say anymore. You older than me twenty years. You must understand life better than me?

You look at me and you say: 'It's like the way you came into my life. I feel as if I am not naked anymore.'

I feel as if I am not naked anymore. That a beautiful sentence.

I listen, I wait. I feel it something you not finish in your sentence, but you not want say it.

So I help you: 'Ok, I come into your life, but you not know if you wanting carry on this with me all the times. You will want to break it and see what can make you move on . . . '

'We will see.' You stop me, and take me into your arms.

'It's important to be able to live with uncertainty.'

intimate

intimate adj having a close personal relationship; personal or private; (of knowledge)
extensive and detailed; (foll by *with*) *euphemistic*
having a sexual relationship (with); having a
friendly quiet atmosphere n close friend

How can *intimate* live with *privacy*?

We have lived together after first week we met.
You said you never lived so closely with another
person before. You always avoided intimate with
the other person. You said to have your friends
more important than your lovers. That's so
different with my Chinese love — family means
everything.

Maybe people here have problems being
intimate with each other. People keep distance
because they want independence, so lovers don't
live with together, instead they only see each
other at weekend or sleep together twice a week.
A family doesn't live with together therefore the
intimate inside of a family disappeared. Maybe
that why Westerners much more separated,
lonely, and have more Old People's House.
Maybe also why newspapers always report cases
of peterfiles and perverts.

★　★　★

103

We are in your old white van. You want to show me somewhere special called the Burnham Beach.

'Is it the British ocean?' I ask, excited to visit sea for first time. You are laughing.

'B-e-e-c-h, not b-e-a-c-h. In English, a beech is a type of tree, not an ocean. I'll take you to the sea another time.'

How I ever understand your complicated language — not even any change in accent like we have in Chinese. We have four intonations, so every tone means different word. Like:

mi in first tone means to close eyes.
mí in second tone means to fancy something.
mǐ in third tone means rice.
mì in fourth tone means honey.

Anyway, on the highway of M40, I have my dictionaries to check out what exactly that *beach/beech* is. *Collins* tells me that is a European tree, but when I look my little *Concise* dictionary, says it is a tree called 'Shan Mao Ju', which grows everywhere in China. We cut those trees for lighting fires in kitchen. We used to carry baskets and collect their nutty seeds when we were little.

The woods are dark, lush, and wet.

Trees are huge, tall, and solid.

The whole woods are growing silently and secretly. The whole woods are decay. On way to woods it was a beautiful day, but inside woods the climate is totally different. Is chilly and rainy. Rain drops from those hundred-year-old greyish branches and leafs, and the rain fills the ponds stuffed by weeds.

In the muddy and greeny pond, lotus gently floats, and the dragonfly dashes. You hold me and caress me. We are in each other's arm. You lift my denim skirt, and you touch my garden. My garden is warm and moist. You stroke my hip, and I unzip your jean. We make love. We make love. We make love under the silent beech tree. So quiet, so quiet. We can hear children on the football field in the distance are yelling.

Only the rain drops, fall on our hair, our skin. Rain drops on the cowslip flower by our feet, without disturbing us.

free world

free world esp. *US* *hist* non-Communist
countries

You say:
'I feel incredibly lucky to be with you. We're
going to have loads of exciting adventures
together. Our first big adventure will be in west
Wales. I'll show you the sea. I'll teach you to
swim because it is shameful that a peasant girl
cannot swim. I'll show you the dolphins in the
sea, and the seals with their babies. I want you to
experience the beauty of the peace and quiet in a
Welsh cottage. I think you will love it there.'
You also say:
'Then I want to take you to Spain and France.
I know that you'll love them. But we'll have to
wait for a while. We need to earn some money.
I'll have to get more work doing deliveries in the
van to boring rich people. Can you put up with
me being so boring — or do you think you'll get
fed up with me after a while?'
Later you say:
'I feel so good about the love that you and I
have with each other because it happened so
quickly and spontaneously, like a forest fire.'
And you say:
'I just love the way you are.'

Everything good so far, but from one thing — you don't understand my visa limited situation. I am native Chinese from mainland of China. I am not of *free world*. And I only have student visa for a year here. I not able just leave London English language school and go live somewhere only have trees and sea, although is beautiful. And I can't travel to Spain and France just to fun — I need show these embassy officer my bank account to apply my Europe visa. And my bank statements is never qualify for them. You a free man of free world. I am not free, like you.

May

custom

custom n long-established activity or action; usual habit; regular use of a shop or business

The café is name greasy spoon, Seven Seas. All windows is foggy from the steam. You order tea as soon as you walk into. Noisy. Babies. Mothers. Couples. Lonely old man. You are opening the newspaper and start drink thick English Breakfast milky tea. And me being quiet.

I want talk to you. But you are reading paper. I have to respect your hobby.

'So where are you from?' I ask handsome waiter in white suit.

'Cyprus.' He smiles.

'Are these chefs also from Cyprus?'

'Yes.'

'So your Cyprus chefs cook English breakfast for English?'

'Yes, we Cypriots cook breakfast for the English because they can't cook.'

I see from open kitchen that sausages are sizzling on the pan. And mushrooms, and scrambled eggs, they are all waiting for being devoured.

I love these old oily cafés around Hackney. Because you can see the smokes and steams coming out from the coffee machine or kitchen

111

all day long. That means life is being blessed.

In this café, there is a television set above everybody's head. The TV on but doesn't have any images, only can hear BBC news speaking scrambly from the white snow screen. It is a little disturbing for me, but it seem everybody in this place enjoy it. Nobody here suggest fix the TV.

Suddenly white-snow-screen changes to green-snow-screen, and the BBC voice continues. A man nearby eating some bacons with the *Daily Mirror* says to the chef:

'That's an improvement.'

'Yes, Sir,' replies the chef. 'Well, at least you don't have to eat your breakfast, read the paper and watch the TV all at the same time.'

'That's true.' The man chew his bacons and concentrates on page with picture of half naked blonde smiling.

I want to talk. I can't help stop talking. I have to stop you reading.

'You know what? I came this café before, sit here whole afternoon,' I say.

'Doing what?' you put down the paper, annoyed.

'I read a porn magazine called *Pet House* for three hours, because I studied English from those stories. Checking the dictionary really took lots of time.'

You are surprised. 'I don't think you should read porn mags in a café. People will be shocked.'

'I don't care.'

'But you can't do that. You'll make other people feel embarrassed.'

'Then why they sell these magazines in every little corner shop? Is also even sold in the big supermarket.'

I believe everything to do with the sexuality is not shameful in West. Do what you like.

The man next to us finishes his bacons, half naked woman photo with huge breasts still being exposed.

'I think I go now buy another porn magazine,' I say, standing up.

'OK, you do whatever you want,' you say shaking head. 'This is Hackney after all. People will forgive you for not being *au fait* with the nuances of British customs.'

You dry up your cup of tea.

fart

fart *vulgar slang* n emission of gas from the anus
v emit gas from the anus

Suddenly the man next table reading newspaper with naked-breast-woman made a huge
noise.

'What is that noise name?' I ask you.

You cannot understand what I mean. Too
much involving in looking house property
advertisement on the newspaper.

I try to explain: 'How to say a word which
represents a kind of noise from the arse?'

'What?'

'You know that. You know it is a wind comes
from between two legs.'

'It's called a fart.'

Fart?

The old man who reads the newspaper stares
at us for several seconds, then buries himself
into the paper again.

I never hear English person says anything
about fart. They must be too shameful to
pronounce that sound. There are lots of words
we used in China so often, but here people
never use it. Even English dictionary say it is a
'taboo'.

'屁' is *fart* in Chinese. It is the word made up

114

from two parts. 尸 is a symbol of a body with tail, and underneath that 比 represent two legs. That means fart, a kind of Chi. If a person have that kind of Chi regularly in his daily life that means he is very healthy. Chi (气), everything to do with Chi is very important to us Chinese. We had so many words related to Chi, like Tai-Chi, or Chi-Gong, or Chi-Chang.

Yes, *fart*, I want remember this word. Is the response means you enjoys a good homely cooking, after big meal. Mans in China loves to use this word everyday.

You are still concentrating on your *Guardian*, something serious about the terrorism. I am talking to nobody. The old man next table sees I am fed up, so says to me:

'I'm off, darling. Do you want my paper?'

He leaves the café but turns his head looking at me again.

I pick the newspaper from his table. There is a headline:

LOST FOR WORDS — THE LANGUAGE OF AN ENDANGERED SPECIES

It is a story about ninety-eight-year-old Chinese woman just died. She is the last speaker of womans-only language: 'Nushu'. This four-hundred-year-old secret language being used by Chinese womans to express theys innermost feeling. The paper say because no womans practise that secret codes anymore, it marks that language died after her death.

115

I want create my own 'Nushu'. Maybe this notebook which I use for putting new English vocabularies is a 'Nushu'. Then I have my own *privacy*. You know my body, my everyday's life, but you not know my 'Nushu'.

home

home n place where one lives; institution for the care of the elderly, orphans, etc adj of one's home, birthplace, or native country; sport played on one's own ground

'I am going to go to see a family nearby, do you want to come?' you ask me.

'Family? What kind of family? Not your family?'

'No. They are Bengalis.'

Is not very normal you want see other family. Because you not really like family concept. You say family against community. You say family is a selfish product.

It seems that you like other's family more than you like your own. In this Bengali family, you know those kids for many years, since you worked as youth worker. In a house, between Brick Lane and Bethnal Green Road, old Bengali mother raises ten children. Is big three-floor house with ten little rooms. Five childrens are from same mother, and another five childrens are from another woman but with the same man. The father, a Bengali married man, came to London twenty-five years ago and remarried to this mother in London. He ran some business between England and Bangladesh.

117

Then he died, left one family in London, one family in Bangladesh. But the five Bangladesh-living children want come to London, so they were brought here living with this London mother. These kids are from three to twenty-four. The youngest one was born in 2000. How strange a child born of that year! He only can say 'bye-bye' in English. The oldest one just graduated from the Gold Smith College. He studied Politics and he wants become lawyer.

'I not understand how mother can raise ten children without a husband,' I say in little voice. 'And she doesn't have any job either!'

'That's why I like this family. They just get on with their life without making any fuss. They have a small business making earrings and necklaces from home.'

'And two groups of children from different mother, they don't fight at all?'

'No. They enjoy sharing life together, not like other families. I wish my family was like this.'

'Do you hate your family?' I ask.

'Well, I don't like them. They are sad people. I broke away from them many years ago.'

You go into silent.

I can't imagine what like to break up with my family. Even though my mother very bad temper and make me pain, my life relies on them, and I can't survive without them.

'Do you want have family with me?' I ask.

'Aren't we a family now?' you say.

'No, a real family.'

'What is a real family?'

'House, husband and wife, then have some

118

children, then cooking dinner together, then travel together . . . '

'I thought the Chinese were supposed to be Communists.'

You seem like making fun. What you mean?

We look at each other, no more discussion on this.

You say *salaam malai coom* to the old mother. The mother, she is covered in old green Sari. Her skin is deep brown and lots of wrinkles on her face. She never any education and never speak one word English. She always smiles and very little talking. When her children talks in English loudly in TV room and watching BBC she just sit there, peacefully watching, like she understand they say. Bathroom flush doesn't work and shower doesn't work. There is not money to fix house. But it seem fine for them. It seem their life is not messy at all. They use cold-water-shower once a week, and they don't use toilet paper because they always use water to clean then tip bucket down loo.

There are drug dealers doing business outside of their windows, and many drunkens pass by with bottles clunkling every night, but the family not get any harm.

★   ★   ★

In Chinese, it is the same word '家' (jia) for 'home' and 'family' and sometimes including 'house'. To us, family is same thing as house, and this house is their only home too. '家', a roof on top, then some legs and arms inside. When you

119

write this character down, you can feel those legs and arms move around underneath the roof. Home, is a dwelling house for the family to live.

But English, it's different. In *Roget's Thesaurus*, 'Family' related to: *subdivision, greed, genealogy, parental, posterity, community, nobility*.

It seems like that 'family' doesn't mean a place. Maybe in West people just move round from one house to another house? Always looking for a house, maybe that's the lifelong job for Westerners.

I keep telling you I need a home. Your face look gloomy, and seem disappointed that you cannot make me happy.

'But I am your home,' you say.

'Yes, but you always move around, and you don't want live in this house.'

'You're right. I'm tired of living in the city.' Then you add, 'I can't see myself getting married either.'

'But I like city and like to have marriage. So that mean we can't have a home together,' I confirm.

'No, I didn't say that,' you say.

You look distant to me.

★ ★ ★

Love mean home. Or, home mean love?

The fear of without home. Maybe that why I love you? The simple fear?

I am building the Great Wall around you and me because I am too scared to lose the home. I been living in that big fear since my childhood.

You barely ask my childhood. To you it a blind

120

zone. When I look back my childhood I realise how violence of my emotional world was.

We were peasants. My parents worked in rice fields. They not making shoes until I graduated from high school. After they understood they never earn money from their fields, they sold fields cheaply, and start making small business. I always being beaten up by big girls. In village people show their emotion by hitting and shouting to each other. My father hit me sometimes, also my mother. That was normal.

We were poor. The food was not enough. We had little meat. I was frightened to eat more than my mother expected in every meal. Occasionally there was some fried porks on the table, and it smelled like heaven. But I dared not to reach my chopsticks to the meat, which prepared only for my father. Man needs meat and man is more important than woman, of course. I looked at pork and my heart was squeezed by the desire. I give away anything for could bite one piece fried pork! My mother always watched out on the table. I hated her, but also frightened by her. She would beat my chopsticks if I reached that pork.

I was hungry all the time, because I never can have something I really wanted eat, like meat, any kind meat. That hunger still remains in my stomach until today.

My mother had very bad temper. Maybe she hated me because I was an useless girl. She cannot have the second children because we have one child policy. Maybe that's why she beated me up. For her disappointment. Life to her was unfair too. She was beated up by her mother for marrying my father. She was deprive everything which belonged to her since she married him.

When I grow up from teenage, I couldn't trust anything and anybody. Maybe I even don't have concept of 'trust' at all. It not existing in my dictionary. First, I couldn't trust my country. We told that we are proud of thousands of years history but next day we saw beautiful old temples being demolished into ruins. All old things have to be demolished and to be cleaned up. Does that mean our past value nothing anymore?

I need make my own home, a home with my lover. But I don't know how keep that home, all the time, for rest of my life. I'm scared I will lose that love. The fear is like poison in the every corner in my heart. That what you dislike.

'You should trust me. I'm not going to fall in love with somebody else,' you say.

'But who knows? I can trust you, but I don't trust when you are seduced by someone,' I say.

'But you have to trust me,' you insist.

'Yes, but that doesn't mean you not fall in love with new person. You can trust me, but perhaps I fall in love with the new person. So what is trust really?'

'Well, if we fall in love with a new person, then that's fine. That's not something we can control.' You look bit cool.

'What you mean that's fine? What you mean we can't control? We can, if we want!' I say, as strong as woman warrior.

★ ★ ★

So we change subject. We know we can't go anywhere. Anything else we can talk under one same roof? Apart from the lovely tea, salad, and learning new vocabularies?

'When is your national day?' I ask.

'Why on earth do you want to know that?'

'Not important day for you?'

'Not particularly. We call it St George's Day. It is some time in April or May, I can't remember.'

I don't know who is St George. Or maybe he is someone like Chairman Mao. I don't want bother myself to know all these dead people.

So we are speechless again.

'So, when is your birthday?' you ask me.

'July 23, but that's not my real birthday. My mother only know my birthday in Chinese moon calendar date and when Western calendar system introduced into our society she forgot.'

'Seriously?' Your face is lighted.

'Yes, we never had birthday cake in our family for ceremony so why you need the date of birth? Only because the official registration,' I say.

'But what about your passport? What date is written on your passport?'

'I wrote any Western date I think of and authority just print it on my passport.' How exciting to you, this subject.

I carry on: 'My father doesn't know his birthday, because his parents died when he was little child. My mother know her birthday is on the fifteenth day of seventh moon, is the day of Hungry Ghost Festival. So all her life is about keeping away from that hungry day.'

colony

colony n group of people who settle in a new country but remain under the rule of their homeland; territory occupied by a colony; group of people or animals of the same kind living together.

The way you make love with me, is totally new experience in my life. Is sex suppose be like this? Penetrating is way for you to enter into my soul. You are so strong. And your strength is overwhelming. For you, I am unprepared. You crush me and press me into your body. Love making is a torture. Love making is a battle. Then I get used it, and I am addicted by it. The way you hold my body is like holding small object, an apple, or a little animal. The force from your arms and your legs and your hip is like force from huge creature living in jungle. The vibrate from your muscle shakes my skins, the beating of your heart also beating my heart.

You are the commander.

You kiss my lips, my eyes, my cheek, my ears, my neck, and my silver necklace. It is like my necklace having a special magic on you. And that magic force you devote yourself to my body. Then you kiss my breasts and you suck them. You are like baby who is thirsty for mother's milk. You lick my belly and my legs and my feet. You possess my whole body. They are your farm. Then you come back to my garden. Your lips are wandering in my cave, and in that warm and wet nature you try find something precious, something you always dream about. You wander alone there and love there and want live there.

My whole body is your colony.

June

prostitute

prostitute n a person who offers sexual intercourse in return for payment v make a prostitute of; offer (oneself or one's talents) for unworthy purposes

I need develop my Western life so I go Charing Cross Road try to find some cooking books. I want know how to make Western food, like pastas, or Yorkshire pudding. I am ended up in Soho Original Bookshop. There are no kitchen books here, apart *How to Make Love and Cook Dinner at the Same Time.* Lots of books here exposing naked body. *Prostitute,* I read this word from one of photo books. The pictures are shocking. I am standing there and reading the whole book. Bodies, strange costumes, strange positions, more bodies having sex together.

★　★　★

Soho, Berwick Street. My feet can't move away from a sex shop. Some leather bras with two hole in middle, some leather belt, some handcuff . . .

A word *loin* written on some instructions, which I never studied before. Standing in front of these shelfs, I check my *Collins* dictionary.

129

Loin n part of the body between the ribs and the hips; cut of meat from this part of an animal pl hips and inner thighs **loincloth** n piece of cloth covering the loins only

There is no more explanation. I hate this dictionary. Where is an exactly *inner thigh*? And what *loincloth* look like? Do people wear *loincloth* everyday?

Putting my dictionary back into pocket, I find shopkeeper stares at me like a tiger. And there are two old mans, both are bald, they stare at me too. I leave the shop.

★　★　★

Red light district.

One, two, three, four, five, six ... I am changing the notes to coins.

I am in peepshow room. It is tiny room for one person to stand, and I can see turning stage through little hole.

I insert the coin of the first pound, and start watching a woman shows her nude.

She is a blonde. Shining hair like golden velvet. She is young. She wears a tight shining top. Her lower body is also covered by piece of shining cloth. Is that the *loin cloth*? Now she uncovers herself. She has a fine round breast, like two summer grapefruits. Her skin is a little dark, like she just coming back from sunny beach.

The peep hole close. I insert second pound. The light turns into red. Now her sex is bathed

130

in redness. She lies down on round stage, which covered by red velvet. The stage is turning, slowly, smoothly.

I insert third pound. She is opening her legs. The legs of white jade. She smiles to everybody; even the place between her legs is smiling. Her garden is flirting with the world around it. She has a rosy garden, which two lips half opened like waiting for the kiss. I never saw other woman's garden before. It shocks my eyes. I remember one day when you and me making love, you give me small mirror to reflect the place between my opening legs.

'That's your clitoris,' you tell me.

'Liquorice?'

I found there my colour of my sex is brown. I never know the colour of my sex before.

I insert fourth pound. Now her hidden place is totally exposed, showing her secret landscape. Then her right hand caress her valley of the tenderness. Her long slim fingers, reaching her sex, are like a beautiful ballet dancer dancing in her garden. She fondles her valley, up and down, gently, and again and again. Two petals blossom in her wet garden. The petals are fresh like rose. Her bush is dark, like a fertile delta, a delta connecting to a secret path. She looks light heated. But her face disappears, only the desire talks to people.

I insert the fifth pound. Now she lays her back on the stage, raising her two legs high above. 阴道 — Yin Dao: the tunnel of darkness, that is Chinese word to say vagina. Her tunnel of darkness is right in front me. Her secret tunnel, winding and curved, is like a maze. Inside of the tunnel is pink and juicy, like an open fig.

The peep hole close off again, and I insert into my last pound. She still there. Her naked body moving on the red velvet. What her name? What her life like? Is there man in her life or lots of mans? Where she from? Serbia? Croatia? Yugoslavia? Russia? Poland?

★ ★ ★

Same day, same afternoon, same alive sex show spot. I change more coins. This time I spent twenty pounds, for watching two persons performing.

Now, on the stage, a beautiful young man and a black hair woman.

The man has a masculine body. He is very fit, and his skin is golden. He wears pair of glasses. He has the beautiful lush hair tied up to a pony tail. He only wears tight shorts, and his legs are strong. He kisses the woman. The woman wears a red bra and a silver mini skirt. Her sweet breasts bulged upwards, inviting those thirsty eyes. The man unbuttons her bra. Her nipples are immediately blossom, like pink rose bud in early summer. He caresses her neck, her breast, her waist, her hip, and her legs. He is so elegant, a young gentleman. But he is a *prostitute — person who offers himself for unworthy purposes*, like the dictionary says.

While I am standing there watching, I desire become prostitute. I want be able expose my body, to relieve my body, to take my body away from dictionary and grammar and sentences, to let my body break all disciplines. What a relief that prostitute not need speak good English. She also not need to bring a dictionary with her all the time.

Now her turn, her power on him. She seduces him. Her hands with scarlet fingernail fondle his delta, a place like a hill covered by the grass. His bird is growing bigger and stronger. And he cannot help to devour her pink nipples, to kiss her snow white neck, and to whisper into her ears. Her body is a ceremony, a power station, a light house. And the neon lights spread the magic colour on her skin.

He becomes impulsive. He lifts her short silver skirt, then I see her delta. She has very lush bush, like bush growing by the river in the tropical zone. His fingers travel through her bushes, and disappeared into her cave. Her face now is lighted. Her mouth is half opened. Waiting and arousing. His fingers come out from her cave. He kneels down, starts to kiss her bush and sucks her cave. Her juice is shining on his face.

The great decadence is attracting me.

The great decadence is seducing me like a magnet.

The music goes to the end part. Big melody. Almost disturbing.

On the turning stage, the man stands like a mountain. The woman kneel down and takes his bird into her mouth. Her lips are as wet as her valley. She sucks him. He is slightly shaking, and his body is swinging. He holds her naked shouder strongly and he endures. Two bodies sticks together. Now he cannot hold her any more. The volcano erupts, and the silver liquid covers her face.

heaven

heaven n place believed to be the home of God, where good people go when they die; place or state of bliss

My father said he once dreamed eating some spring sprouts. My father loves spring sprouts. In that dream his teeth bites the fresh spring sprouts and he clearly hears the crispy sound from his mouth. It is such a beautiful sound. It is just like heaven, he said. But my mother always disagree with him. My mother think there is no sound in the dream. If you hear sound in the dream just because you imagine you hear it.

'The dream is silent, like heaven.' That what she said.

Chinese Heaven must have lots of peach trees, lots fairy ladies dressed in silk skirt with long sleeves, like we saw in the martial art films. There is no mans, but only the son of the Heavens lives there, eating peaches everyday, served by beautiful fairy ladies. I don't know if this Heaven where my grandmother prayed and wanted to go after she died. I hope so. But if my grandmother really living there now, then she would ruin the whole fairyland. Because she is ugly.

'Is Heaven really silent?' I once asked my mother, timidly.

135

'What?! You think Heaven is as noisy as this compound?' she answered.

The compound we lived was crowdy, tiny and messy like war zone. There were about twenty families live with us, and every family had seven or nine children since One Child Policy only starts from 1977. So there were about 150 children constantly shouting fighting crying everyday. Then there were about twenty grandmothers shouting to at least forty sons and forty daughters-in-laws every evening. So compound is like little village. And we raised roosters and hens everywhere in the compound too. All the time you can hear little chickens snivelling for being stepped when kids ran over them. And fathers would chase kids and beat the kids up. That was the life before my parents start make business. Soon, leather shoes, cloth shoes, sports shoes were piles and piles like hill sitting in our compound yard. At the beginning they worked for some shoes buyers. Five years later my parents opened their own factory, and then everybody from the same compound became their employees.

★   ★   ★

So you, a Westerner, ask me again: 'What do you think Heaven is like? Assuming you think there is one . . . '

I recall what my mother thought of Heaven and what my father thought of spring sprouts. I am confused: 'Which Heaven? Chinese Heaven or Western Heaven?'

'Is there a difference?' you laugh.

'There must be different.'

'If there are different Heavens, I guess then the different Heavens might fight each other.'

'Fighting is good. Makes Heaven more liveable,' I say.

You look at me surprisely. You know I like to fight. I am woman warrior. I like to do everything through fighting. I fight for everything. Struggle for everything. We Chinese are used to struggle get everything: food, education, house, freedom, visa, and human rights. If no need struggle then we don't know how to live anymore.

romance

romance n fantasy, fiction, legend, novel, story, tale; exaggeration, falsehood, lie; ballad, idyll, song

Friendship endures longer than romance. I often think this sentence in your diary, but when I look in *Thesaurus* I see so many possible words for *romance*. Is *romance* love?

'What is exactly *Romance*?' I ask you.

'Romance?'

You are thinking hard. Maybe is first time people ask this question to you.

'Well, it's a complicated word ... Maybe romance is like a rose ... '

'Rose? What kind of rose?'

We are in garden so you go back in house fetch book.

'A rose like in this poem,' you say, and read me:

All night by the rose, the rose,
All night by the rose I lay.
Dared I not the rose steal,
And yet I bore the flower away.

Poem very beautiful, I want know who wrote it. On book says Anon.

'This Anon very good writer,' I say. 'I think I prefer to Shakespeare, much easier.'

You laugh. 'Yes, and perhaps even more prolific.'

'?'

'*Anon* isn't a person. It's just what we say when we don't know who wrote something.'

Annoyed about this Anon, I look round in your garden. There is no any rose, let alone Chinese rose.

'How can you never plant any rose in the garden?' I say. 'Every *green finger* growing rose in this country, as far as I can see. You should have one.'

You agree with me, this time, no any doubts.

So we now have a climbing rose in our garden, against the wall. Is a skinny plant with five green leafs and some annoying thorn. We had argument in flower market because I want buy rose with blossoms, but you rather buy little sprout and wait for its growing.

You use your favourite tool — *spade* — to dig the hole. 'The hole must be twice as wide as the root spread, and two-feet deep . . . ' You measure the hole with the fingers: 'The rose has mainstructural canes and flowering shoots, so the canes must be tied or woven into a support to keep the rose off the ground.' You are so scientific. I look at you. Are you *romantic farmer*?

Then, here, in new world far away from my home, here, under your fruit tree without flowers, you start sing a song, a famous song

which I heard somewhere maybe in China
before. You voice gentle and almost trembled.

Some say love it is a river
   that drowns the tender reed
Some say love it is a razor
   that leaves your soul to bleed
Some say love it is a hunger
   an endless aching need
I say love it is a flower
   and you its only seed

It's the heart afraid of breaking
   that never learns to dance
It's the dream afraid of waking
   that never takes the chance
It's the one who won't be taken
   who cannot seem to give
And the soul afraid of dying
   that never learns to live

When the night has been too lonely
   and the road has been too long
Then you think that love is only
   for the lucky and the strong
Just remember in the winter
   far beneath the bitter snow
Lies the seed that with the sun's love
   in the spring becomes the rose

If people hears this song, and she doesn't feel moved
— then I think that people must not human.
   I love you. And you know I love you. And you
love me as well.

You tell me song is from Bette Midler — your favorite. You say you like the strong, rude women. You say all homosexual like Bette Midler, Mae West and Billie Holiday. But Billie Holiday not strong — she commit a suicide.

* * *

Two days after, you take me watch documentary films double bill. Two crazy women in one night.

Small cinema on Rupert Street. First one about Mae West, an extremely successful Hollywood star, always make audiences happy and laughing. She is a 'No. 1' woman without any 'competition' in the world, as she said to media. Sexy, always wearing shining jewellery, flirty, confidently. Even in her eighty-seven years old, she dressed a sexy white dazzling fur coat, and all around by young black bodyguards and cameras. And her face still very beautiful and young even in that age. She the tropical sun, nobody can be more brighter than her.

Second film is *Billie on Billie*, right after Mae West documentary. First scene in the film is Billie Holiday standing on the stage sadly singing, 'Don't talk about me . . . ' — last appearance on TV before she died. She is a extremely sad face, hopeless expression. From the film I learned her struggled by her childhood, her prostitution mother, her sex abuse when she twelve years old, her drug and alcohol, her poor dignity being a black. Billie Holiday, she is not melancholy, she is hopeless.

'I always fear . . . ' she says in the film. A

141

strange fruit. I want leave the cinema to cry. I feel her pain in my heart. And later on when I think of Mae West again I find her story is so surreal, like fairy story comes from the moon . . .

I want become Mae West, be her courage, her bravery, her humour, her creativity, her challenging to the world. She live with admiration, rich, and confidence. Men all her slaves; men used by her. I want play that role. But is the reality I am nobody, not even painful Billie, I am just obscure nobody with name starts from Z. Maybe this *romance* with you put some weight into my life.

July

physical work

physical adj of the body, as contrasted with the mind or spirit; of material things or nature; of physics

For six days now London really hot. Suddenly people almost nudes in street and sit about on grasses chatting. Mrs Margaret changed to beige suede sandals. I can't concentrate her lessons in the heat.

Hotness make you unhappy because you must drive van like oven.

I see you always disappear with that white van. A very old van with a side door sunken and another side door cannot close *properly*, unless you kick it violently. The front and the back windows always covered by thick dust. It is a peasant van, or a working-class van.

The van is your business method to earn money via delivering goods. You say you can get this job only because you have got a big van.

You drive whole day in that van for delivering. The goods are for somebody's birthday, party, ceremony, wedding, or any day someone has excuse to consume the money.

You drive from 7 o'clock early morning, till late night. You drive seven days a week. Every day on the road, on those roads towards middle-class big family houses.

You come back home in the dark, without any energy left. Life suddenly becomes bit boring. I find you are a physical man, a labourer, using your hands to survive. While lots people in this world just need use fingers to earn living by clicking computer keyboard.

I never see you sell the sculptures. Nobody want buy a suffered and twisted statue, I guess. If they do, they maybe buy a female nude statue. Once I saw you were making a wooden swimming pool model, as the advertisement for Red Bull company. Another time I saw you were making a huge telephone model for Vodaphone. I heard you saying 'it looks ridiculous', 'it is so tacky' while you were making these things. But you got paid. Then one day you stop getting these kinds job. I don't know why.

★   ★   ★

'You always say physical work makes people happier, but you are not happy now.' I make some tea and salad for you. It is so late.

'I am too tired. That's why . . . ' You sit on the chair, by the kitchen table. You hair is messy, covered by the dust.

'Physical work doesn't do any good,' I say.

'But at least you don't worry about living.' You sip the tea, the tea is sucking your energy.

'For me mental work better than physical work,' I say. 'Nobody wants physical work. Only you, and my parents.' I put the salad bowl in front of you.

You start to eat salad, and the room goes quiet. The white cabbage is very crunchy, and the red carrots are hard too. Your teeth are trying to grind them into pieces. Your face looks uneasy.

In my hometown, we don't use these two words:

Physical work / mental work

All the work is called 讨生活 — scavenge the living. Making shoes, making tofus, making plastic bags, making switches . . . All these works rely on our bodies. And bodies earn our living back. Now I come to abroad studying English. And I do that with my brain. And I know in the future I earn living from my brain.

You insist physical worker better than intellectual.

'An intellectual can have a big brain, but a very small heart.'

I never heard before that. Why you think of that?

'I want a simple life,' you say. 'I want to go back to the life of a farmer.'

Intellectual: 知识分子 (zhi shi fen zi)

知识 mean knowledge, 分子 mean molecule. Numerous molecule of knowledge will make up man knowledgeable.

In China, intellectual is everything *noble*. It mean honour, dignity, responsibility, respect, understanding. To be intellectual in China is splendid dream to youth who from peasant background. Nobody blame him, even in Culture Revolution time and seemed these people suffered, but really was time for them having privileged to being re-educated, get to know another different life.

147

So if you don't want to be intellectual, then you a Red Guard too, like Red Guards who beat up intellectuals during Culture Revolution. A Red Guard who living in the West.

I never thought I would like a Red Guard, but I like you. I am in love with you, even if you say you not intellectual.

I not intellectual either. In the West, in this country, I am barbarian, illiterate peasant girl, a face of third world, and irresponsible foreigner. An alien from another planet.

isolate

isolate v place apart or alone; *chem* obtain (a substance) in uncombined form

You are not at home again. You have so many social contacts, so many old friends need to see and chat, so many ex-lovers live in the same city as well, and I don't know anybody in this country. I am alone at home. Dictionary checking, checking dictionary . . . I am tired of learning words, more new words, everyday. More exercise on tense, make a sentence on the past participial tense, and make a sentence on past conditional tense . . . So many different tenses, but only one life. Why waste time to study?

The garden outside is quiet. The leafs are breathing and figs are growing. Bees are beeing around the jasmine tree. But I feel lonely. I look that male nude statue under the fig tree. He is still facing down, like always. An enigma. Totally an enigma. Whenever I go to the modern museum, like Tate Modern, I never understand those modern sculptures. I hate them. They seem don't want to communicate with me, but their huge presence disturb me.

The house is empty. Is the loneliness an emptiness?

I remember my grandmother always recite two

149

sentences from the Buddhist sutras:

色不异空，空不异色。

色皆是空，空皆是色。

She explains it means the emptiness is without form, but the form is also the emptiness. The emptiness is not empty, actually it is full. It is the beginning of everything.

So far, I don't see the emptiness is the beginning of everything. It only means loneliness to me. I don't have a family here, and I don't have a house or a job here, and I don't have anything familiar here, and I only can speak low English here. Empty.

I think the loneliness in this country is something very solid, very heavy. It is touchable and reachable, easily.

The loneliness comes to me in certain hours everyday, like a visitor. Like a friend you never expected, a friend you never really want be with, but he always visit you and love you somehow. When the sun leaves the sky, when the enormous darkness swallow the last red strip in the horizon, from that moment, I can see the shape of the loneliness in front of me, then surround my body, my night, my dream.

Something missing, something lost in my life, something which used to fulfill in my China life.

We don't have much the individuality concept in China. We are collective, and we believe in collectivism. Collective Farm, Collective Leadership. Now we have *Group Life Insurance* (集体人寿保险) from the governments as well. When I was in middle school, we studied *Group Dancing*. We danced with 200 students as part of the school lesson. We have to dance exactly the same pace and the same movement in the music. Maybe that's why I never feel lonely in China.

But here, in this place in the West, I lost my reference. And I have to rely on my own sensibility. But my sensibility toward the world is so unclear.

I take out one a book from your shelf, Frida Kahlo. That Mexican woman artist. It is a picture album of her painting, her life, and her terrible illness, being disabled after the bus accidents. So many self-portraits. I thought one painter only does one of these in his life, like one person only have one gravestone. But Frida Kahlo has so many self-portraits, as if she died many many times in her life. There is one called *Self-Portrait with Necklace of Thorns*. She has the sharp and heavy eyebrow like two short knives; her eyes like black shining glass. She has the thick dark hair like a dark forest; the necklace of thorns climbing on her neck. There is a black monkey and black cat sitting on her shoulder.

The impression on her face is so strong. I learn that she had to plant metal in her body so that to support her survive from disable. I feel my heart is being penetrated by the thorns she painted. I feel painful.

When I put down Frida Kahlo, I think of you. You love the heaviness of life. You like to feel the difficulty and the roughness. I think you like to feel the weight of the life. You said you hated

151

IKEA, because furnitures from IKEA are light and smooth.

I walk to the garden, staring at your sculptures again, one by one, carefully, attentively, thinking of you with my new eyes. That naked man, without head, stubbornly faces down towards the ground with twisted huge legs. What makes him so suffering?

humour

humour n ability to say or perceive things that are amusing; amusing quality in a situation, film, etc; state of mind, mood; *old-fashioned* fluid in the body v be kind and indulgent

Yesterday at home we celebrate my birthday. I turn to 24. OK I don't know when is my real birthday, but passport birthday can be great excuse to have a big Chinese meal.

It is the year of goat. My animal sign is goat too. It is my second twelth year after the year of my birth, which means I am having my most important year in my life, because it is a year I meet my destiny. My mother will say that.

We are having a hotpot birthday party. You say you never eat hotpot meal before. You say it is interesting to see people sitting around a big table and cook food from a steaming pot in the middle.

So there is about six or seven people all together. Some are your friends. Two of them from my English language school. One is from Japan called Yoko. Yoko has very slim cat eyes, and neat cut fringe covered her forehead like a hat. Her hairs has lots different colours like red and green and blue. She looks like punk, or maybe she is real punk. Another one is from

Korea called Kim Yan Zhen. Kim has very pale face, and she looks whiter than any white people. These two are famous in our language school because their English is impossible. Mrs Margaret say my English even is better than them. I think maybe because when Japanese girl speaks English, people would think she is speaking Japanese. And when Korea girl speaks English, she keeps nod her head and bow her back to show the modest, but without giving anything verbal. But anyhow, they are kind of my comrades, although Korea hates Japanese, and Japanese were not friendly with Chinese. Most important thing, they use very simple words. Yoko sits down and say, 'Are we eat?'; Kim Yan Zhen looks at the hotpot and asks, 'Cook, you?' I like that. I like people speak that way. So we understand each other easily.

It is a meal between East and West, though three Orientals only can speak foreign language to communicate.

It is *worship* of eating, is the exactly word to describe this.

I make spicy red chilli soup for the hotpot, by putting in gingers, garlic, spring onions, leeks, dried mushroom and chillis to stew the soup. After the soup becomes boiling I put in tofu and lamb. With hotpot, lamb is essential for the soup. It gives the form content. Otherwise hotpot is the interesting form of meaningless. Is a pity that you are *vegetarian*, and all of your friends are also *vegetarians* in this room.

While I am cooking the lamb in the pot, you

and your friend just look at it, and put the uncooked carrots straight into the mouth. In Chinese, we say the way you cut the meat reflects the way you live. They must be timid people.

Here is the birthday gift from you. Two book. The first is *The Happy Prince and Other Tales* by Oscar Wilde. You say is good book for me to start with, to understand English writing easily. The second one is *To the Lighthouse* by Virginia Woolf. You say it can be read later on, when my English becomes very good.

Then Japanese girl Yoko gives me small little box. It is delicate, like perfume box. On the cover it says:

Waterproof Personal Massager

MADE IN CHINA

What's this waterproof? Battery? Watch? There is picture on the cover: it is something looks like small cucumber but slightly bended.

Curiously, I open the box. It comes out a smooth plastic thing look exactly like small cucumber. On the bottom there are some buttons: on/off/fast/slow. Is it toothbrush machine? I put into my mouth, but it not fit easily. A massage machine for facial beauty? Or for back and neck aching? Maybe the instruction will tell me.

I unfold the little piece of instruction.

Natural Contours — it's great to be a woman

Then there is a printed letter:

Dear Customer,
Thank you for purchasing your new natural contours massager. Natural contours is a revolutionary approach to personal relaxation: a massager that's ergonomically designed to fit the contours of a woman's body. It is our goal to offer you personal products that encompass quality, taste, and style to please today's woman.
With the move toward greater self-awareness and exploration for women, we hope this product meets with your expectations and opens up a whole new world of personal relaxation for you.

Then there are some sincere advertise on the verse of the page:

Answering the call for quality personal products, natural contours delivers unbeatable performance: a stylish massager with a low noise motor that provides stimulating vibration. The elegant, impact — resistant casing is ergonomically designed to complement a woman's natural shape.

TO OPERATE: SWITCH TO 'ON' POSITION

So follow this instruction I switch on the machine. It is beeping. Everybody who eats the hotpot now stops eating and look at me.

You lean to me and whisper in my ear, 'It's a vibrator. You put it in your vagina.'

Holding the vibrate, my hand is shaking badly. I switch it off. It makes me feel horrified.

Everybody in the party laughs.

'I think Asian people have a great sense of humour,' you say.

'No, we don't,' I clarify.

'Why not? You and Yoko make everybody laugh all the time.'

'No. We Chinese don't understand humour. We look funny just because the culture difference, and we just being too honest,' I say.

'Yes, when you say things very honest, people think you are funny. But we stupid,' Yoko adds.

'Yes, I agree.' Here comes Korea girl Kim Yam Zhen eventually. She barely speaks, but whenever she speaks she impress everybody. She seriously makes a comment:

'Humour is a Western concept.'

Gosh, is super English. I didn't know Kim's English improve so much recently.

Your friends look at us three Orientals, like look at three panda escape from bamboo forest.

I watch the vibrate. I want to make a comment as well: 'Enjoy sex is a Western concept too.'

'That's rubbish. Mans enjoy the sex everywhere,' says Korea girl Kim Yan Zhen.

Mans look at each other.

'But, I mean, Yoko, did you give her the vibrator as a joke or as a serious gift?' you ask.

'Of course serious,' answer by Yoko. I know Yoko is serious. Oriental people are serious, even young punks.

'Have you never seen a vibrator before?' one of your friends ask me.

'No. How would I?'

'But it's made in China,' the friend says.

157

'Doesn't mean I see it,' I say. 'Actually those big international co-op factories run by foreigners. And the managers employ lots cheap labours like peasants, peasants' wives. And those womans they don't really know what is this machine for, but they just make it, by putting every piece of spare parts together. It is like they make computers by putting pieces together, but they never ever use computer.'

Why it doesn't say 'Dildo' or 'automatic sex for woman' on the box? Maybe because it made in China, not allow to say things so clearly. It might become a big scandal if somebody from his village know his neighbour making plastic cocks everyday in a factory. Or maybe these factories are secretly protected by the government. Because Chinese government say there is no sex industry in China.

Putting more white cabbages into the hotpot, I can't help thinking about those womans waking up early every morning to make vibrators. I am seeing them leaving behind their unemployed bad-temper husbands and poor children to sit on production lines and make vibrators. And those peasant womans will never use the vibrator in this life. All they want to know is how much they will earn today and how much money they can save for the family.

I put back this plastic cucumber into the box. When I leave it on the oily table, I see the warning from the side of the box: *clean with washcloth and mild soap.*

migraine

migraine n severe headache, often with nausea and visual disturbances

Another hot day. You left home in the morning with your old white van. I went to school and I had an exam on vocabulary. The exam went OK. I think I gain more English words since I have been lived with you. Mrs Margaret praises me. She said I a fast learner. She doesn't know I have been living with an English man every day and night. Soon school will end for summer holidays. My parents not expect there be so many holidays when they paid this school.

I come back home in the evening and switch on BBC Radio 4. I know my listening comprehension still bad. I hear *Six O'clock News*, then *The Party Line: comedy about a frustrated MP*. I don't understand English comedy.

I am waiting for you to be back.

You come back home almost ten. You hug me with a cold wind. You look so frail. You look painful. You say you got two parking tickets today, one is forty pounds, another one is sixty pounds. You say you were fighting with the traffic policeman who is a black. You say why black people they are so kind and friendly in Africa, but are so rude as long as they live in London. You say London is a place sucks. You say London is the place making everybody aggressive.

You say you got strong headache again, and your whole body aches as well.

I make you some tea. Your favourite peppermint tea. (On the tea bag it says: produce of Egypt. I thought English people they produce their own tea.) I poured the boiled water into the pot. It is an old teapot in brown colour. It is ugly. You say you used this teapot for almost ten years. Ten years, you never break it. Is unbelievable.

You drink the tea and you stare at the steam from cup.

I give you a painkiller pill. You take it. But you look worse. You move your body to the bathroom. You throw yourself up.

It is unbearable. I hear your pains, through the closed bathroom. It feels like you are throwing up all the dirts from your body, all the dirts from the sick world.

The running tap is being switched off. You come out from the bathroom, with a pale face.

'I never had headaches before I came to London. My body was so healthy when I lived in the country with my goats, and I was just planting potatoes. Since I moved here I'm struggling all the time. My body is in misery. That's why I hate London. Not only London, all big cities. Big cities are like huge international airports. You can't have one moment of peace here, and you can't find love and keep it.'

But what about the love between you and me?

It happen in the big city, London, a very international place, like airport. Can you keep that love? Can we keep it? I ask myself, in my heart, touching your hair. There is something shaking inside me.

Now you lie down on the bed, your body is hidden in quilt. Your quilt is so heavy, and the texture feels very rough. Not right for this hot weathers. It must be with you for many many years, and it must be from somebody else — you never buy beddings. When I saw your quilt and sheets the first time, I just know you lived long time on your own without a woman. A house has a woman will definitely have a soft and cosy beddings.

Feeling your body is shivering in pain, I can't leave you there. I take off my clothes, and I lie beside you.

'Will you have sex with me?' you ask me, with a weak voice.

'Why? Do you want?' I am very surprised.

'Hmm.'

Your hand still presses your head where is the pain from.

'If I come it helps me forget about the pain and fall asleep,' you say.

'But what if nobody beside you or you don't have a lover when you are very ill?' I am shocked.

'Then I would do it with my hand. Like I did before you came into my life.'

I don't know what to say anymore.

Touching gently your little bird, I move my fingers. I can feel your pain directly. Your pains is like electric current transfer into my finger, then

161

my palm, then my body, then my head. I become shivering with my anticipation, for that I want cure your pain.

You face look relieved, but your breath becoming much heavier. Your little bird gets harder in my fist. I don't feel sexy at all; all I wish is to stop you suffering.

'Are you ready to come?' I am holding you.

'Yes . . . ' you say, enduring the great pain of climax.

Your body is shaking. Then the sperm comes. My hand is completely wet. It jets, again and again. The milk. It must be bitter milk when a person is suffering. It is the milk of love, my love to you, but it is also the milk of pain, your pain in your life.

Your breath calms down. You are leaving your pain.

We lie still, without moving even for one centimetre. We are just like your still statue. The sperm on my palm is drying. You fall into sleep. I can feel every single pulse on your wrist. I can feel every single beat from your heart. I breathe in your breath. I inhale your exhale. It is being so long that we lie here like two statues. I look at your face, for so long. I even can see your death. The shape of your death.

August

equal

equal adj identical in size, quantity, degree, etc;
having identical rights or status; evenly balanced
n person or thing equal to another

Rupert Street, fish restaurant. Saturday evening.
Large lobster placed on the window is so
seductive that I can't move my feet away. We get
in. You order goat cheese, and extra vegetables. I
order fish soup and squid BBQ in wine. We agree
having two glasses white wine as well. Later,
when waiter gives the bill it forty pounds all
together. Expensive.

You take out twenty pounds, put on the bill
book. I don't move. I look at you, wondering.

'Half!' you say.

'Why? I don't have twenty pounds with me!' I
say.

'You've got a debit card.'

'But why?'

'I'm always paying for you. In the West, men
and women are equal. We should split food and
rent.'

'But I thought we lovers!' Loudly, I argue.

The old couple next table stops eating, look at
me with strange face.

'It's not about that. You are from China, the
country with the most equal relationship

165

between men and women. I'd have thought you'd understand what I'm talking about. Why should I pay for everything?'

I say: 'Of course you have to pay. You are man. If I pay too, then why I need to be with you?'

Now you are angry: 'Are you really saying you're only with me to pay your living costs?'

'No, not that! You are man and I am woman, and we are live together. When couple is live together, woman loses social life automatically. She only stays at home do cooking and washing. And after she have kids, even worse. So woman can't have any social position at all. She loses . . . what is that word . . . financial independence?' These are what I learned from Radio Four Woman's Hour every morning ten o'clock.

'Really? OK. So, if the woman stays at home all day, like you, why can't she hoover the floor? Why do I have to do the hoovering after I've done a whole day's work?'

That's true. I never woover the floor. I only sweep the floor. And my eyesights is very bad, so there are always lots things left on the floor.

'But I wash clothes! And I cook everyday!'

'Thank you, that's very kind of you. But what's wrong with a bit of hoovering?'

'Because I hate that woover. You must pick it from the rubbish place. It is so noisy, and it is so huge. It is like dragon. I just don't like something so big!'

'Come now! You like a big cock, don't you, so why don't you like a big hoover!'

'!'

OK, so woman and man pay half half even

166

when they live together. And woman and man have their own privacy and their own friends. And woman and man have their own separate bank account. Is that why Western couples split up so easily, and divorce so quickly?

We argue all the way back to home. Open the door, make a pot of tea, you start woover the floor again.

So noisy. It makes me headache immediately. The woover must be invented by mans. I sit on chair not let the big dragon swallow me and take out the Little Red Book from my drawer. There are some pages about womans and *equal* in Mao's speech:

In order to build a great socialist society it is of the utmost importance to arouse the broad masses of women to join in productive activity. Men and women must receive equal pay for equal work in production.

This must be the original thoughts which became legend 'womans hold up half of the sky' in China.

While I am in deep thought about China, you switch off the dragon. You stare at me, and say:

'I wish I'd never given you books. Now all you do is sit there reading and writing. You've become so *bourgeois*.'

frustration

frustrate v upset or anger; hinder or prevent

You lie in bath. The water comes to top, and the bubble covers your body. We both always take bath when we feel depressed. Do most English people do that, especially in the long dark winter? I wonder. How many baths we have been taken since we being together? In last six months the bath I had must be more than I did in the last twenty-four years.

Now, you even didn't switch on the radio. You lie there like a nude statue in the water.

'Why you are silent?'

You shrug your shoulders. Have no comments.

You don't want talk. Not at all. Not even one word.

'Have you got headache?'

You shake your head.

'So you don't want talk to me?'

'No.'

'Why not?'

'I just want to be on my own to think. You know people sometimes just want to have their own space.'

Only your face is on the surface of water. Impression of your face is like the sky being covered by a big piece of dark cloud. You not happy.

168

'Why you not happy? What have I done wrong to you?'

'I just feel tired of you,' you say. 'Always asking me words, how to spell them, what they mean. I am fed up.'

I listen.

'It is too tiring to live like this. I cannot spend my whole time explaining the meaning of words to you, and I can't be questioned by you all day long.'

You come out from bath, covering your body with that blue towel. You are so cold to me. You leave me there alone.

I feel like being *abandoned*. The word I learned the first day I arrived London in the bloody red Nuttington House. It is the second word in my *Concise Dictionary*, coming after *Abacus*.

You carry on:

'It is so hard for me. I don't have my own space to think about my sculptures, my things, and my own words. I don't have time to be on my own. Now when I talk to other people, I become slower and slower. I am losing my words.'

I listen. Gosh, I am upset to hear this. I have to say something to defend myself.

'If so, that is not my fault. It is just because we live in such different cultures. It is very difficult for both you and I to find the right way to communicate.'

You listen, then you say: 'You really are starting to speak English *properly*.'

After this, the evening we are in the world of

169

silence. I don't want ask you any words anymore, at least not in several hours, and I tell myself I shouldn't talk to you either, at least tonight. You not want talk to me. The air in the house becomes heavy. Finally you say to me: 'Come with me to see a film.' I take my jacket and I follow you. We are driving the white van to the cinema. Oh, cinema saves our life.

★   ★   ★

Yes, maybe you are right. Words maybe not really the first thing in life. Words are void. Words are dry and distant towards the emotional world.

Maybe I should give up learning words.

Maybe I should give up writing down words every day.

nonsense

nonsense n something that has or makes no sense; absurd language; foolish behaviour

我真他妈地厌倦了这样说英文，这样写英文。我厌倦了这样学英文。我感到全身紧缚，如同牢狱。我害怕从此变成一个小心翼翼的人，没有自信的人。因为我完全不能做我自己，我变得如此渺小，而与我无关的这个英语文化变得如此巨大。我被它驱使，我被它强暴，我被它消灭。我真想彻底忘记这些单词，拼法，时态。我真想说回我天生的语言，可是，我天生的语言它是真正的天生的吗？我仍然记得小时侯学汉语的同样的苦功和痛楚。

我们为什么要学习语言？我们为什么要强迫自己与他人交流？如果交流的过程是如此痛苦？

I am sick of speaking English like this. I am sick of writing English like this. I feel as if I am being tied up, as if I am living in a prison. I am scared that I have become a person who is always very aware of talking, speaking, and I have become a person without confidence, because I can't be me. I have become so small, so tiny, while the English culture surrounding me becomes enormous. It swallows me, and it rapes me. I am dominated by it. I wish I could just forget about all this vocabulary, these verbs, these tenses, and I wish I could just go back to my own language now. But is my own native language simple enough? I still remember the pain of studying Chinese characters when I was a child at school.

Why do we have to study languages? Why do we have to force ourselves to communicate with people? Why is the process of communication so troubled and so painful?

Editor's translation

discord

discord n lack of agreement or harmony between people; harsh confused sounds

Forgot since when, we started to fight.

We fight everyday. We argue everyday. The sound in this house is *discord*. Fighting for a cup of tea. Fighting for the misunderstanding of a word. Fighting for the ways I like to add the vinegar in the foods but you hate it. Fighting for the freedom as you think it is important more than anything else.

Argument expands onto every possible direction:

Typical argument 1:
(On Tibet)

'I remember you saying that Tibet belongs to China. I can't believe you can think that.'

'Well . . . You see things from a white English's point of view. Shame that your English failed to colonise Tibet and China,' I throw back.

'But now Tibet is colonised by the Chinese!' You raise your volume.

'If Tibetan is not with Chinese, then it ruled by British Empire, or American anyway. Because

Tibet never really been economically indepen-
dent! They always need rely on others, rely on
powerful government. Since China and Tibet are
in the same piece of land, why we two can't be
together?'

'It depends what you mean by 'together'! It
can't be at the cost of Tibetan culture. And look
how many Tibetans you've killed . . . '

'I didn't kill any Tibetans! No any other
Chinese I know in my life killed any Tibetans! In
fact, nobody in China wants go to that desert!'

'But the Chinese government killed Tibetans.'

'Yes, of course BBC news only report bad side
of China.'

Typical argument 2:
(On food)

'It is boring eat with you everyday. You only eat
vegetable, no wheat, no pasta, no white rice, no
bread, only goat cheese, let alone any fish.
Hardly any restaurant suits you. And not very
much fun for my cooking either. My parents will
say you lose the most joyful thing in your life.'

'Well, you are the enemy of animals. How
many animals do you think you have killed in
your life?' You fight poison with poison.

'Eating animals is the human nature. In the
forest, tiger eats rabbit. Lion eats deer. That's
how the nature works.' That's how my teacher
said in my middle school.

'But you Chinese eat anything, even endangered
species. I bet if dinosaurs roamed the forests of

174

China, someone would want to see what dinosaur meat tasted like. How come you people have no sense of protecting nature?'

'But what so different of eating plants? Everything has its life. If you are so pure, why not just stop eating? So you can have no shit?'

'You are impossible to talk to!' You stand up, leaving the dinner table.

Typical argument 3:
(On career)

I say I want to be a great English speaker among other Chinese. And I want to do something big in my life and get fame.

'You're so bloody ambitious. What's the point of fame? Why not just try to be yourself.'

'Why ambitious is not a good thing?' I ask.

'Well, for a start, it makes you pretty difficult to live with,' you say.

These words hurt me.

'OK, so I have big ambitious, and it ugly. But why you want to show your sculptures to others? You should just make your own thing and never show it to people!'

'I want to show the sculptures to others because I am curious about what they might think. I'm curious about their reactions. I don't care about being someone big. I don't care about fame or money.'

'That because you are a white English living in England and you own the property and you have social security. You are boss of yourself, so you have dignity. But I don't have anything here in your country! I have to struggle to get these things!'

I am almost shouting, but I should not shout in your private property. People call policeman to come anytime in this country.

identity

identity n state of being a specified person or thing; individuality or personality; state of being the same

I try to be quiet with you in the house. I have been reading books you gave to me. I quickly finished Oscar Wilde's *The Happy Prince and Other Tales*. I loved the nightingale story. It was so sad. Nightingale's love not being valued by the prince at all. Why beautiful story always is sad? And I loved the selfish giant who has a huge garden too, but the last sentence made me cry. It goes like this: 'And when the children ran in that afternoon, they found the Giant lying dead under the tree, all covered with white blossoms.' I start reading *To The Lighthouse*. You are right, it is quite difficult for me. On the back it says it is about a middle-aged woman with her eight children in a summer house. Eight children without any husband? Gosh, it must be a hard book. I holding breath while read the first page. I can't breathe freely because there are hardly full stops. Virginia Woolf must be a very wordy person. The writing is so forceful, is nearly painful for me to read. I suddenly understand that you must be suffered a lot from me, because I am so forceful and demanding on words too.

And even worse, you are forced to listen my messy English every single moment. You are unlucky to be my lover.

I put down the book and leave it for my future reading.

I am being caught by the word '*identity crisis*' on *The Times*. I write it down into my notebook. I always want to find this word, now here I encounter it. Now I want think about my own identity, in an *intellectual* way.

My mother told me: 'Your skin too dark and your hair too thin. You don't look like me and your father at all. You are like your barbarian grandmother!' She said to me: 'Look at your big feet. A real peasant's feet! Nobody will want marry you.'

I hated her, and I wished she could die immediately.

But she is right about this: so far nobody really wanted to marry me.

When I was in middle school, my schoolmates always laughed at me. So I spend time on reading to avoid talking to them. I read *Snow White And Seven Dwarfs* in Chinese, and I saw my mother is as evil as that stepmother queen. But I didn't have a snow-white skin and I was just a peasant girl. So there was no prince will come save me and that's my destiny. Being a teenage I was dying to run away from my hometown, the town which my mother always beat me up and blamed me for everything I have done wrong, the place without my dream and my freedom.

The day when I arrived to the West, I suddenly

realised I am a Chinese. As long as one has black eyes and black hair, obsessed by rice, and cannot swallow any Western food, and cannot pronounce the difference between 'r' and 'l', and request people without using *please* — then he or she is a typical Chinese: an ill-legal immigrant, badly treat Tibetans and Taiwanese, good on food but put MSG to poison people, eat dog's meat and drink snakes' guts.

'I want to be a citizen of the world.' Recently I learned to say this. I *would* become a citizen of the world, *if* I have a more useful passport. Ah Mrs Margaret, that conditional again!

anarchist

anarchist n person who advocates the abolition of government; person who causes disorder

'What is *Anarchist*?' I raise my head from *Guardian*.

We are in 'First Choice', a cheap greasy spoon, forty pence for a cup of tea. We like this kind of places. They don't ask us leave if consumption less than £1 after one and half hour. I love east London.

You have an earl grey tea, and I have coffee. Liquidish eggs flow everywhere on my plate. Kids nearby are crying — two crying baby with one fat mother, no husband again.

Frown gathers on your forehead.

'Anarchists? Anarchists don't believe in government. They think society shouldn't have a ruling government. That everybody should be equal.' You answer, slowly.

'Sound like Communist,' I say.

'No. Communists believe the working class can control the power of the whole society, but Anarchists don't believe in any power. They are very individualistic, whereas Communists believe in the collective.' You stop describing, as some working class man looks at us, stop biting his sausages.

180

My interests being aroused. I want to discuss more. You are my academy.

'But sounds Anarchist is the end of the Communist, or the advanced Communist. Is target or triumph of the Communism revolution is that, through the revolution wiping out the difference of the classes and eliminating the ruling government. No country boundaries. So the world can be *equal*. Am I right?'

'Maybe.' You open another page of paper.

'So are you an Anarchist?' I am not giving up.

'I was an Anarchist. But not anymore.' Now you give up your paper, and answer me seriously. 'Most Anarchists are in fact bourgeois. They don't really want to give up any advantages. They can be very selfish. I don't think I am that kind of person now. I want to give up material things, and live the simplest possible life.'

The simplest possible life is the most complicated thing to achieve I say to myself.

'So who are you?' This time I really want to know.

'I don't know. Maybe an *atheist*. I don't believe there is a god living in the sky. I don't believe in Capitalism, but I'm also not convinced by Communism, the way it is now.'

'So do you believe in anything?' I ask.

'Hm,' is your only answer. 'What about you?'

'Me? I do believe there is a kind superpower control all our life. It is also the power above the nature. And this superpower human being cannot really do anything to change it.'

I look outside of the window, and I am sure right now in this very right moment there is a mysterious superpower above us, above our cheap café and above our silly conversation.

You point the ad of *Donnie Darko* in the paper and ask me: 'Have you seen this film? The teacher in it says to Donnie: 'You are not an *atheist*, you are an *agnostic*.' I think you are an *agnostic* too.'

'What is *agnostic*?' I am searching my little *Concise Chinese-English Dictionary* in my pocket.

But after we both look at the dictionary up and down there is nowhere we could find the word *agnostic*. Maybe this is the word not important to Chinese. Or there is no *agnostic* in old time of China at all. Or maybe it is a very capitalism word that's why the authority censored it?

'An *agnostic* is someone who believes in a spiritual world, a metaphysical world. But he hasn't found what he should believe in yet . . . '

'Wait, what is 'metaphysical'?' I open my notebook.

'Metaphysical means not physical, not real . . . ' A pause, you say: 'but I think you might be a *sceptic*.'

'What?'

Again, I pick up my dictionary and open it immediately. I am in a hurry to learn. I am in a hurry to understand all these words!

While I am burying myself in the sea of words in the dictionary, you say, 'Honey, your English is good, but not *that* good. I have to say.'

The working class man in the nearby table chews his kidney pie, looking at me with enormous wonder. I think I make his day.

hero

hero n principal character in a film, book, etc; man greatly admired for his exceptional qualities or achievements

You feel happy again, your mood is like English weather.

You are in the peace, like the fruit tree without flowers in the garden. You are happy because you start to make a new sculpture. So now dirt and mess everywhere in the house. It is like living in a construction site. Clay and plaster and wax and water. Your happiness is from your own world, from your physical object, from the molded male head, male arms, male leg, male attraction . . . Your happiness is from your masculine world, and in that world you feel everything is under the control.

Your sadness actually is nothing to do with me. Your stress is not really from me. It is from your masculine world, because you don't feel satisfied with your life as a man. And you might think I am an obstacle in your life. You think your sadness caused by our relationship, by love prison. It is not true. Your happiness and your sadness is from the world that you fight with yourself.

My love to you is like a lighthouse, always

searching something special about you. And you are special. But I don't know if you think me in the same way. You always say things like these to me:

'How did you burn the rice again? A Chinese woman shouldn't burn rice, you eat it everyday'

'I spend more time with you than with my friends. Why do you still complain? What else do you want?' . . .

It seems you don't treat me as a special person in your life. You treat me as one of your friends. And there is a line you draw between you and me. There is a limit, from your heart, from your lifestyle, which makes love feels like a friendship. You live inside of me, but I don't live inside of you.

You said Frida Kahlo is one of your heroes. Of course I knew that. I knew that from your book shelf. I knew that because I knew your heroes are always in pain, and died of young.

In nobody's London Fields, I sit on a chair, and read about Frida Kahlo again. I want understand you, and I want understand your twisted nude lying on the ground of your garden.

Frida, her body falling apart when she was alive. Her bones were being smashed by the bus accident. Death had been eating her everyday until one day nothing is fresh left. Again I see your naked man lying down on the ground. Your twisted statue, how similar to Frida's body in her painting.

In your world, I am losing my world. In your pain, I am losing myself. Everything makes me thinking about you, only about you and your world. I am like a wallpaper stick on the wall of your house, looking at you and decorating your life. 'Don't bury me, burn me. I don't want to lie down anymore,' Frida lay on the bed and said to her husband. She could not move one inch. A negotiation between her and the devil. My life compare with hers, is nothing.

freedom

freedom n being free; right or privilege of unlimited access

我说我爱你，你说你要自由。

为什么自由比爱更重要？没有爱，自由是赤裸裸的一片世界。为什么爱情不能是自由的？难道爱情是自由的监狱？那么多人活在监狱里头吗？

I say I love you, but you say you want to have freedom.

Why is freedom more important than love? Without love, freedom is naked. Why can't love live with freedom? Why is love the prison for freedom? How many people live in this prison then?

Editor's translation

schengen space

The 'Schengen space' is the territory constituted by the countries which are members of the Schengen agreements. The following countries are today active members of the Schengen agreements: Austria — Belgium — Denmark — Finland — France — Germany — Greece — Iceland — Italy — Luxembourg — the Netherlands — Norway — Portugal — Spain — Sweden. The aim of the Schengen agreement is to allow free circulation of people within the territory of the member countries.

All foreigners who are legally resident in one of the Schengen member States can make short visits without a visa in any other member State, provided they travel with their valid passport which must be recognized by all the Schengen States and a resident permit issued by the authorities of the country of residency. Since the UK is not a member of the Schengen agreement, nationals who are not exempted from visa requirements by the Schengen member states and who reside permanently or temporarily in the UK need a visa to enter the Schengen Space.

'Have a look at this,' you say. 'If you got a visa to go to France, you could go and see all these countries.'

You pass to me leaflet.

I read carefully terms of the 'Schengen Agreement'. I don't know where is Luxembourg, where is the Netherlands, Norway or Finland,

and I of course don't know where is Greece. I thought Greece is in Rome. After I check the European map, I read it again the terms. I understand wherever I want to go I need visa, but I still don't understand what is 'Schengen'. Me, a native mainland Communism Chinese, a non-EU member and non-British passport. For visa application I need prepare my medical insurance paper, my financial document (thanks that I have a free accommodation here from you, so I save lots of money from my parents prepared for my renting).

'So much trouble, I don't want to go,' I say. 'I want stay in Hackney with you.'

You look serious. 'I think you should see a bit of the world without me. After all, you've never been to the sea.'

'So, you take me.'

You only smiling. 'I think it's important you go by yourself.'

★ ★ ★

When visa arrive I am still doing research on European map, trying to understand where is where, like Poland is next to Germany, and Romania is above of Bulgaria. But I couldn't find Luxembourg.

'Don't worry. Just buy an unlimited Inter-Rail ticket, then you can take the train to wherever you want in Europe,' you say to me, very experienced.

'Unlimited?' I am so excited to know this.

'Yes, you're under twenty-six, so the ticket will

189

be cheap. You'll get to see the whole of the Continent.'

'Continent? Where is that?' I ask.

'You'll know where the Continent is when you come back.'

You talk to me like I am your child. Maybe I am like idiot in front of you. Maybe you love the idiot.

You take out some old maps from your bookshelfs. There is map of Berlin, map of Amsterdam, map of Cologne, map of Rome . . . You blow the dusts on these maps, and put in my bag.

'Now they are useful again, after all those years sitting on the shelf,' you say.

'But all these places must be changed from the time you went,' I say, thinking of map of Beijing every month being changed.

'It's not like China,' you say. Then you take a novel called *Intimacy*, author Hanif Kureishi, and put into my bags too. 'This is for you to read on the train.'

You sit down on the chair, having tea, and looking at me packing.

I already feel lonely when I put my shirts into the rocksack. Is that all you want? Want me away from you?

September

paris

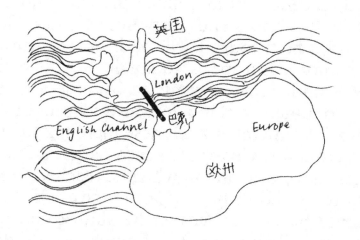

I thought English is a strange language. Now I think French is even more strange. In France, their fish is *poisson*, their bread is *pain* and their pancake is *crêpe*. Pain and poison and crap. That's what they have every day.

'Du pain?'

The man serves me in a small brasserie nearby Les Halles, with some bread on the little basket.

'Non. Je ne veux pas pain!' I answer. I learn this from *French for Beginners* by Michael Thomas.

But one minute later, he comes back with a small basket of pain again, asks me:

'Encore un peu de pain?'

'Ça sufficient!' I say, wiping my mouth, stand up.

No more pain in my life.

Only rice makes me happy.

193

Journey London-Paris was big let down. When I sit on the comfortable chair in the Eurostar, the French-accent-staff announce the whole journey will take two hours and thirty five minutes. Gosh, two and a half hours I will be in the centre of a new country. Europe is so small, I can't believe it. No wonder that it wants to become a Union. I am so much looking forward to see English Channel. I remember a Chinese man in 2001 who swam cross this Channel to earn national face for Chinese government, but when he reached French seashore he didn't have visa to arrive. Of course he didn't have visa, because he almost naked. In China, we all thought that French people don't understand Heroism. Hero doesn't need visa. Even a third world hero. Chairman Mao used to swim cross Yang Zi River, biggest river in China, in his very old age. He is of course, a hero.

The train is fast. There are still green fields and white sheeps outside of window. The speaker announce that in five minutes we will be in the tunnel of English Channel. So exciting, I can't wait. Five minutes later I find we are in the absolutely darkness, deep darkness. I thought the tunnel is made of glass, so it is transparent to be able to see the blue seawater. But there is no difference with London underground. In the long darkness, I wonder if those fishes beside us are blocked by the tunnel and will be confused in the sea. Disappointed, I am finding myself come out from the dark tunnel, and arrive to the French side.

★   ★   ★

Musée D'Orsay, Paris, a place exhibit lots of work from *Impressionists*. I-m-p-r-e-s-s-i-o-n-i-s-t, and I-m-p-r-e-s-s-i-o-n-i-s-m. Longest two words I have ever learned so far. Even longer than c-o-m-m-u-n-i-s-t and c-o-m-m-u-n-i-s-m. There are several paintings from Monet. I stare at these obscure water lilies, obscure gate, and obscure sunrise. The colour and the subject in these paintings are like somebody looking through a dirty window glass. Especially the one about the impression of sunrise, sunrise on the sea. Everything blurred, the wave, the sea, the sun, the cloud are all blurred. Even the colour is blurred too.

★   ★   ★

Night in a cheap hotel. Forty-five euro including breakfast. The room is so small, like a place for one of Snow White's seven dwarfs, but the French-style balcony is always better than English one. I sit on the old high-back-chair thinking there must be one thousand dead people used to sit on this chair and spent their hotel time doing strange or boring things. Turn on the desk lamp, I start to write you a letter. But my eyes can't see anything clearly today; especially I can't read clearly the trails of my writing. White paper too sharp for eyes, black ink too weak to read. When I look at the dictionary, every word is blurred. The optician in London told me the power of my short eyesight is

195

growing, getting worse. They said I can't do laser surgery because my corneal are too thin. Will my future is a world of blurness?

I look out of the window. I can see the black clouds at the bottom of the dark sky, and I can see the dim lights in somebody's house which is not far away from this hotel, and the shadow of trees by the street light. But that's all, no more details in the street.

I remember once you told me about an American eye doctor, who invented Bates Method. He taught those short-eyesight-patients how to use eyes *properly*. He said keep your vision centered. When you regard an object, only one small part should be seen best. This is because only the centre of the retina has the best vision for detail. Rest of retinal area is less able to pick up fine detail. Does this mean I don't or can't use the centre of the retina to see things *properly*? That I like Monet, Van Gogh and all these impressionists, see the world blurred too?

I want to see *you* only at the centre of retina and everything else blurred. What am I doing in this busy Continent when I just want see you?

amsterdam

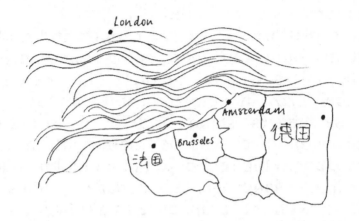

I only stop in Amsterdam for one day. I am going to Berlin. I don't know why I don't feel like to stay. I don't know anything about Holland, and I even didn't know *Holland, Dutch, the Netherland* meaning the same place. Why a country have so many different names? Before I thought these three spread somewhere differently in Europe.

There are only two things I know about Holland: first, the Communist Dutch man Joris Ivens made a film called *The 400 Million* about Chinese against Japanese invasion; second, all the tulips in China are said from Holland. About Joris Ivens, I saw a film camera been exhibited in the Museum of the Revolution in Beijing. It is the camera he gave to the Communists army at late 1930s. Maybe that's why Chinese Communists started making films since then.

197

Amsterdam Central station. A large place. A place for temporary stop and for passing by.

So many people here, but nobody will stay here more than one hour.

From platform 15 to 1, I cannot find a place to sit my bum. No, there is no single chair or bench in this Central Station. The passengers hold their pizza in hand and eat it without a seat. The passengers stand and drink paper-cup coffee without a seat. A man, with a huge suitcase and a big rocksack, talk in mobile phone in a strange language. A language without any similarity with other language I have heard in my whole life. He keeps talking in the phone and his face is sad. He talks in the phone for so long, and it seems like he is being sucked by the telewave and disappeared in the phone-zone. In that dark phone-zone it is no seats either.

The train to Berlin will be departure at 8.15 p.m. Five hours to wait. I decide go for a walk.

Outside station so much water. And houses like doll house. In front of one house I meet a man drinking coffee on doorsteps. I stopped to look at house because I saw some familiar leaf with special fragrant. Lush wisterias climbing on a big tree. I always love this plant. It is so Chinese. It was growing everywhere behind our house in my home town. And it is growing in your English garden as well. I put down my heavy rocksack and try to have a rest.

Man on doorsteps looks at me and asks in

English, 'Would you like a cup of coffee before you start walking again?'

'Oh. Is that convenient for you, to make a cup of coffee?'

He smiles. 'It's no problem. I've already made a pot. So I just need to fetch a cup for you.'

He goes back inside of house. Quite dark inside.

We sit on doorsteps and drink a very bitter coffee without milk. I dare not ask him about milk, thinking maybe Dutch man doesn't use milk.

'I am Peter. And you?'

'Zhuang Xiao Qiao . . . Well, just call me Z, if you want.'

'Z?' he laughs. 'That's a strange name.'

In England, people tell me if somebody says something 'strange' means they don't like it. So I don't answer him.

Then he asks me:

'Are you Japanese? Or Philippino? Or maybe Vietnamese? Or Thailandese?'

I a little annoyed: 'Why I couldn't be a Chinese?'

'Oh, are you?' he says, and looks at me meaningfully.

His smile reminds me of you. A bit different. He wears a black leather jacket.

'Do you like plants?' he asks me, because my eyes were still on the wisteria.

'Yes, I like those vines, wisteria. It is originally from China,' I say.

'Oh, really? I didn't know that.'

He starts to look at the plants as well.

'My father told me that wisteria is very long-lived,' I say. 'Some vines surviving 50 years. They climb the trees and they can kill the trees.'

'You know a lot about plants.' He looks at me: 'So why are you running around the world?'

'I don't know.'

'China is far away from here. And you don't have anybody travelling with you?'

I nod my head. Not knowing what to say.

People in the street are in a hurry with their bags, they must rush back to have dinner with their family. Everywhere people live in the same way.

'And are you going to the train station now?'

'Yes.'

'Where are you going?'

'Berlin.'

'Berlin. A nice city. Have you been there before?'

'No.'

'Berlin is cool.'

But I don't want to know about Berlin, I think only of my *home*. So I ask, 'Do you live in this house? Is this your home?'

'Well, not exactly my home. But I rent it.'

'Can I ask what do you do here?'

'Me? I just came back from another country. Cuba. I was there for ten years.'

Cuba? Why Cuba? Live there for ten years as a Dutch? Is he also a Communist like Joris Ivens?

I start to watch him, instead of watching the people in the street.

His eyes meet my eyes.

I look up his home. It is a beautiful old house.

'Don't you want to change your ticket? Then you could stay with me for a bit until you want to go.' He looks at me sincerely. He is very serious, I think.

I shake my head. I put my empty coffee cup on the stone step. I look at my rocksack in front of me. I stand up and ready to go. But suddenly my tears come out without me noticing.

The man is surprised. He doesn't know what to say. He gives me his hand and lets me hold it. I hold his hand, tightly. I don't know him, I don't know him, I tell myself.

* * *

Now the big clock on platform shows 20.08. There are seven minutes left. Sky is pink outside. Waiting and feeling lonely. Now there is no time I can go back to the centre of city.

A big train station is a bleak place. This station is bigger than any station in London. Waterloo Station, King Cross Station are just too normal compare with this one. Travel alone, makes me feel sad when I see all these couples hold each other's hand and wait patiently.

A floating dust, that must be how God see a little human *drifting* on the Earth.

I feel difficult without you. I become language handicapped. I got so many problems to understand this world around me. I need you.

Holding the ticket to Berlin, but I don't feel like to go. There is no one I can meet in Berlin, and there is nothing I know about Germany. I just want go back to London, to my lover.

201

Home is everything. Home is not sex but also about it. Home is not a delicious meal but is also about it. Home is not a lighted bedroom but is also about it. Home is not a hot bath in the winter but it is also about it.

The speaker on the platform renounces something loudly. It is 20.09. The train will leave in four minutes. I look around and ready to get on train. Suddenly, somebody is running towards me. It's him. The man offered me coffee in front of his doorsteps. He is running on the platform, and he is running towards me. I am stepping into the carriage, so I drop my bags on the floor and come out the train again. He stops right in front of me, breathless. We stare at each other. I hug him tightly and he hugs me tightly. I bury my head into his arms. I see my tears wet his black leather jacket. The smell of the leather jacket is strange, but somehow so familiar.

I am crying: 'I don't want to go . . . I feel so lonely.'

He hugs me, even tighter.

'You don't have to go.'

'But I have to go,' I say.

The bell rings. The train starts to move. When his back disappears off the platform, I dry my tears. It is so strange. I don't know what has been happened on me, but something has happened. Now it is over. It is over. I am leaving Amsterdam. There is no way to return. I know I am on a journey to collect the bricks to build my life. I just need to be strong. No crying baby anymore. I pull down the windows, and sit down on my seat.

berlin

'The size of China is almost the size of the whole Europe,' my geography teacher told us in middle school. He drawed a map of China on blackboard, a rooster, with two foot, one foot is Taiwan, another foot is Hainan. Then he drawed a map of Soviet on top of China. He said: 'This is Soviet. Only Soviet and America are bigger than China. But China has the biggest population in the world.'

I often think of what he said, and think of how at school we were so proud of being Chinese.

* * *

It seems that I can't stop to keep meeting new people. When I was in London, I only know you, and only talk to you. After left London to Paris, I was still in old habit and didn't even talk to a dog in Paris. English told that French are arrogant they don't like speak English. So I didn't try talk to anybody in France. But that's good for me. I don't even need to remember how to speak Chinese there. After Paris, I tired of museums. No more dead people.

Opposite my seat a young man in his black coat and red scarf is reading newspaper. It is of course foreign language newspaper. And I don't know the writing of that language at all.

Young man in black coat with red scarf stops reading the paper, and gives my presence a glance then back to his paper. But very soon he stops his reading and looks at the views outside of the window. I look at the window as well. There are no any views. Only the dark night, the night on no name fields. The window reflects my face, and my face observes his face.

Only him and me in this small carriage.

'Berlin?' He asks.

'Yes, Berlin,' I say.

We start to talk, slowly, bits by bits, here and there. His English speaking accent not easy understand.

'My name is Klaus.'

'OK. Klaus,' I say.

He waits, then he asks: 'What is your name?'

'It is difficult to pronounce.'

'OK.' He looks at me, seriously.

'I am from China, originally,' I say. I think I

should explain before he asks.

'Originally?' he repeats.

'OK, I have lived in London for several months.'

'I see. I am from East Germany.' He stops. Then he says, 'Your English is very good.'

Very good. Is that true? If it is, he doesn't know how mad I have studied English every day, and even now, on the trip.

So, on this train, this new person, Klaus. He is a stranger to me. Train is really a place for films and books to set up the story. And I can feel me and this man we both want to talk, to talk about whatever.

He says he was born in Berlin, east of Berlin. He says he knows everything about East Berlin, every corner, every street. How lucky, this train is leading to his home, his love.

The night train is moving slowly. It is certainly not a fast train. Only non-important passengers would take this train, or holiday maker.

We lie down opposite each other on the couches in the tiny carriage of the train. A strange position, lying there, he and me. We talk more about Berlin.

He says that he is training in Diplomatic Department in Berlin. Before that he was a lawyer. He wanted to change his career and to live in abroad. He says he used to have for eight years a girlfriend who lives in B-a-v-a-r-i-a (B-a-v-a-r-i-a, he spells slowly to me). He explains it is in the south of Germany, but of course I don't have any idea where is this B-a-v-a-r-i-a. He tells me his girlfriend one day came to Berlin and knocked his door. She told him she wanted to finish this relationship. So he finished it in pain, as she decided. And he decided to change his life and go to work in other countries. I understand Klaus's story, I understand that feeling want to be far away from the past. I tell him I understand him.

Also I tell him about you, the man who I love so much, and the man who makes sculptures in London. I tell him my feeling about you — and how you tell me I have to travel alone.

We talk, then sometimes no words, and just listen.

Eventually the sun comes outside of the window.

'We are getting there,' Klaus says.

★ ★ ★

Gosh, Berlin has a heavy colour, big square buildings. Like Beijing.

'So where you will stay in Berlin?' he asks.

'Don't know. Maybe YMCA youth hotel, because I can have discount from my Europe train pass.' I show him my pass.

'I can take you to a YMCA near my flat, if you want.'

'That's very kind of you. Please. I don't know anywhere.'

'No problem,' he says, and pulls down his luggages from on our head.

I take my rocksack and follow him, just like a blind person.

The early morning air feels cold, like autumn

206

coming. Occasionally, one or two old mans in a long coats walk aimlessly in the street, with the cigarettes in their lips. Under the highway there is bridge. By the bridge there is a sausage shop, lots of large mans queue there to get hot sausages. Gosh, they eat purely sausage in the morning! Even worse than English Breakfast. The morning wind is washing my brain, and my small body. This is a city with something really heavy and serious in its soul. This is a city which had big wars in the history. And, I feel, this is a city made for mans, and politics, and disciplines. Like Beijing.

Then I see the flag, drifting on top of a massive building on a big square. Three bars: black, red, and yellow.

I ask Klaus: 'Is that your country's flag?'

He is surprised: 'You know nothing about politics?'

I admit: 'Yes, I am sorry. I never know it. So many different flags, they confuse me.'

He laughs: 'But you're from China. Everything in China is about politics.'

Maybe he is right. This is a man must know this world very well.

'So it is the German flag?' I guess.

'Yes. It is.'

I stare at the flag, stare at this black red yellow bars.

'Why the black bar on top of the flag?' I ask. 'It looks so dangerous!'

He laughs again, but then stop. He raises his head and looks up the flag as well. Maybe he thinks I am not so stupid.

Black bar of flag is powerful and heavy blowing on top, and I feel a little bit scared. In a reasonable designing, the black bar should be at the bottom, other wise . . . it might cause bad luck. It might cause the whole country's unfortunate.

As I remember, there is another country also has black bar on national flag, which is Afghanistan. But even Afghanistan put the black bar on the bottom instead of top.

I look up the sun through the flag, and the flag seems like a dark spot of the sun.

Through Alexanderplatz station, we are heading to east Berlin. I follow him, like a blind man following a stick. It is seven in the morning. We stand in front the YMCA Hotel. The door is not opened yet. We ring the bell. A man comes opening the door with his sleepy eyes, and he tells us that there is no vacancy until this afternoon.

So we leave YMCA, with our luggages. Standing in the middle of the street, Klaus says I could come to his flat if I want. Is very close to here.

'OK,' I say.

Klaus flat is very tidy. White plain wall, double bed with blue colour bedding, bare wooden floor without carpet, white-tile-pasted bathroom, small tidy kitchen with everything there, writing table with a leather chair, wooden wardrobe and a book shelf. That's all.

No woman's make up or perfumes in the bathroom. No any sign of woman anyway.

He makes a pot of coffee in his small kitchen.

No milk, he opens the fridge and says. We drink the coffee, and he puts some sugar in. I don't want any sugar. I can see there are only a piece of sad butter and two boring eggs in his fridge. He says he will leave Berlin next year, then start his diplomatic job. He grabs a pen and writes down address of flat and nearby tube station. And he gives it to me. Don't get lost he says.

Then he opens the wardrobe and changes his tops. There are at least twenty different colour's shirt and ten different ties hanging inside. And it seems they are all being ironed by someone *properly*. Who ironed his clothes? He puts on a grey-silver-colour-suit, and a dark-red-tie.

'You can leave your bags here, so you can walk around in Berlin. I'll be back this evening from work.'

So I say yes, yes, yes to him, to Klaus. He seems nice man, no harm, only warmth. I can trust him. We walk to bus stop where goes to his office. Several office man and woman in suits and with black leather bags also waiting. Then the bus immediately coming. He kisses on my cheek and says see you tonight at home. It is so naturally, just like in a Western TV, a husband says goodbye to his wife every morning when he leaves to work. I see him disappear with the bus. And I have a strange feeling towards him.

Now I am alone, wandering around in the city of Berlin. I feel really naked. I care about nothing of this city. I have no love or hate whatsoever towards this city.

What I should know about Germany? The Wall? The Socialism? Or the Second World War?

The Fascist? Why they hated Jews? Why Auschwitz is not set in their own country? The history text book in China told us a little about Germany, but very confusing.

I only know they have sausages, different taste sausages sold under the bridge. And people eat the sausage with a wooden stick in the street. I remember this morning a very noble-looking man in front of sausage shop, and was eating tomato-sauce-covered-sausage with his office files under his arm. That's my understanding of Berlin.

It remind me so much of Beijing. The city is in square shape. Straight long street, right, left, no wandering. And some more bigly square building blocks. It must need a dictator like Chairman Mao to make a city like this. But of course this city look much more older than Beijing. Big buildings in Beijing came out from last fifteen years — or I would rather say: last fifteen days. Most of trees standing in Beijing streets are new trees, which being planted maybe no more than five years. History in Beijing doesn't exist anymore, only empty Forbidden City for tourists taking photos.

I pass by that sausage shop under bridge again. The steams come out from the food. It smells good. It seduces me to want have some sausages too. I give three euros to the man in the shop, and he kindly gives me a big pack of hot sausage, with green mustard and red sauce by the side. It look exactly like a lump of shit. But it tastes good.

My body is in Berlin, but my heart is left in

London, left for you. I don't feel myself together. All I want do is find some internet café write emails. I cannot stop thinking of you.

You wrote me from London this morning, or maybe you wrote from last night:

'*Although our bodies are separated, I still feel as if I am with you.*'

I write to you back immediately. I say it is too lonely on the road on my own. I don't see the point.

But you write me back:

'*In the West we are used to loneliness. I think it's good for you to experience loneliness, to explore what it feels like to be on your own. After a while, you will start to enjoy solitude. You won't be so scared of it anymore.*'

I read this email again and again in internet café not knowing your exactly meaning.

In café by big street I go and sit read some pages of *Intimacy* hoping it make me feel close to you. The cheese cake I just had is sticking on the cover of the book. It is very depressed book, I don't understand why you want me to read. It is about a middle-aged man leave his wife and children, to abandon his family life. Is that how you feel living with me? Is that the reason you sent me off to travel the Continent explore my solitude? I feel angry. I put down book, looking around the room.

Is a modern café, the red and black colour chairs and tables are all in geometry shape. So much designing here, it almost feels uncomfortable. I want you suddenly turn up in front of me, and take off my clothes and squeeze my body and hold tightly. Oh, I want to make love with you, make love with you right now, right here. Only making love can wipe out this loneliness. Only making love can touch the soul. I want you hold my body painfully tight. I feel hurting when you squeeze my body like that, but at the same time I feel contented. It's strange. Pleasure could be so painful.

I wander around for whole day. In the big shopping mall watching people. In the stagnant park watching people. In the meat market watching people. Lots leather here on people's clothes. Even in the Starbucks, the sofas are leather sofas. How come so much leathers being produced in this country? A long day of leatherness. Sit and walk and dream. Eventually it comes to the evening. I walk back to Klaus flat. Yes, no mistakes, the exactly right street, and the exactly right gate, and the exactly right door number. Because I got this Berlin map from London, from you. I wonder when you have been to Berlin and where you stayed. Your life before is twenty years ahead of me. No wonder you have so many stories, so many secrets.

I press the doorbell, nobody comes. Again, and again, I press it. Then the door opens. Klaus looks terrible. His body leaning against the door and his knees almost reaching the floor. He falls in front of me.

He is in high fever. He vomit often. He has diarrhoea. He spits out when he comes back from bathroom. He is terribly ill. He even vomit up on bed before he rushes to toilet.

I am so scared. What happened? Did he eat

something bad? Will he die? Although I only know this man nine hours on night train, I have small responsibility to his life now. But what I am going do?

I sit on his bed and give him a glass of tap water. He drinks but straight goes to bathroom to spit out. He lies down on bed again, and says sorry to me. I hold his hand. I lie down beside him and feel his body is like burning. Then he rushes to toilet again. Vomit, till nothing can be taken out from his stomach anymore.

'Give me a piece of paper, and a pen,' he says.

I find pen and paper on his table.

'Please, go out and buy me this kind of water, with a red star and a lion on the label.' He writes down the name of the water:

I can't believe what he wrote! What a German! Water can have such a complicated name!

I come back with four big plastic bottle of water. He drinks. *Gerolsteiner Stille Quelle.* Slowly. Then he lies back to the bed, half sleep. I return to bathroom to fetch a wet towel, and fold it to put on his head.

It is very late, and I am hungry. The man lying on the bed is breathing difficultly. I open fridge and decide boil the only two eggs. Finding the pot, filling the water, switch on the gas, putting in the eggs . . . Look, I can make something in this German kitchen, though it's uncomfortable to cook in some stranger's home. There are some tea bags there, so I make tea. I add some sugar this time, as I am too hungry.

After eating two eggs with salt, I come back his bed. I feel his temperature is still rising. I get up to find his telephone. But I don't know which number I should dial. 999? 911? 221? 123? Is Berlin system like London or China? I give up the telephone and come back to him. I take out the sweat-soaked towel on his forehead and cool it again in the cold water. I am thinking one moment he was so tidy like his bachelor's flat, but another moment he is so messed and fucked up. I don't understand Germans. I switch off the light and lie down beside this man.

I feel so tired by walking around in Berlin whole day. I pull over bits of his duvet to cover my body. Quickly I fall into my dreams.

I am waking up by his heat. It is so hot. He is sweaty and everything on the bed is wet and sticky. He says something not clear:

'Can I have some water . . . ?'

His breathe is heavy and difficult, like he is running at the end of a marathon.

Then he says: 'I feel very very cold.'

I find another duvet in his wardrobe. But now I am too hot under both these duvets. I take off all my clothes, only have my pants left. And I get into the bed again. Underneath two covers of duvet, he hugs me, but still shivering. I let him

214

hug me. I see my leopard-pattern bra lying on the floor, and I feel a bit strange.

His face turns to me, and murmurs, very unclear:

'Stay with me . . . '

I hear him. And I am not sleepy anymore. He lies beside me, with the fever. I hug him. He holds my naked body.

We sleep like this, so close, until next morning . . .

★   ★   ★

The second day, he is feeling better, but is too weak go out. I tidy the bathroom, flush the toilet, and clean the tissues by the bedside. He drank three bottle of water since last night, now only one bottle left. I make some tea, and add some sugar in his cup. My rocksack is still on the floor, without opening it yet.

'Do you know last night you said something to me?' I want to remind him, to find out.

'I'm afraid I can't remember much about last night. My mind was blown up. I must look like shit,' he says, a little embarrassed.

'So you don't remember anything about last night?' I am bit disappointed.

'I remember I asked you to buy some water. And you looked after me. Thank you so much. I thought I was going to die.'

'That's OK. I was a bit scared, actually.'

He drinks his tea, slowly. I don't know what do next. Should I leave? Should I stay? I feel like want to stay with this man.

'Do you think maybe I should spend more time in Berlin?' I ask. Gosh, I wish I didn't ask like that. I hate myself.

'Well, I don't know. It is your decision. Look, thank you so much for everything you did, especially considering you don't even know me. The thing is, I have to go to the office this afternoon . . . '

He looks distant to me from last night.

'Do you think you might come to London one day?' I ask, keep hating myself.

'I don't know,' he says vaguely.

'What about China?'

'I think that's very unlikely . . . ' He laughs.

There is no reason for me to stay here in this bachelor's flat anymore, not even stay in the city of Berlin. I will leave Berlin right now, immediately.

I send you a postcard:

My dearest,
I am leaving Berlin. I really want to go down to somewhere more warm. I don't know if I like to travel on my own. I see all the lovers and families on the train they travel together on their holiday. For me it is not a holiday, it is something like homework from you to me.
I wish you are happy.
Love,
your Z

It is a postcard with the picture of Berlin Wall. Messy drawing everywhere on the wall. It is ugly.

Sitting on bus to station, I can still smell my

body having sweat from Klaus fever last night, and I ask myself: Did I fall in love with him? I don't know Klaus, the man in east Berlin, but I feel close to him. Look, now I have my own privacy, and I don't know if I would tell you when I come back to London.

venice

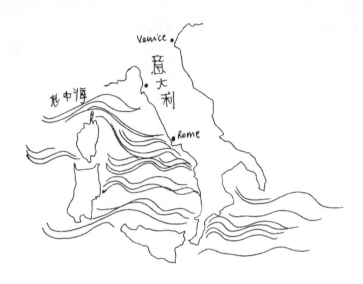

I arrive in Venice after hours and hours sleeping on train. Walk out from station, there are waters everywhere, or say, river, or should say canals. I don't know if these waters are part of sea. But it is midnight, and very dark. Bad time. It mean I have to pay a hotel for over night staying, and I don't know where am I now. I hope I can search twenty-four-hour café to kill the night before the morning starts, then I can find hotel for tomorrow more easy.

On the wall of St Lucia train station, there are some posters hanging there, both in Italian and English, and also in characters like India language. The English says: 'Venice Asian Art and Culture Festival'. I notice it is during this week. That a good thing for me. There are several people also just coming out from station, and looking in map. They argue something on the map, probably argue in Italian, or maybe French, or maybe some other Europe language I not understand.

A man in that group comes to me: '*Parla Italiano?*'

I shake my head.

'English?'

'Yes,' I answer.

'Do you know where is the party?' He looks friendly.

'What party?' I say.

'You are not here for this Asian festival? There is party tonight. We are going there now. I hope it's not too late.'

The man speaks very unclear English, but he seems very keen on Asian.

'No, it won't be too late. It will be too early,' one of his friends says.

'Come along with us if you want,' the man says. 'We can get you in.'

I am hesitating. Should I go? If I can't find that twenty-four-hour café it could be a solution.

'Maybe I come later?' I say, putting on my heavy rocksack.

'OK,' says the man. 'If you decide to come just tell them you know Andrea Palmio and they will let you in.' His friends are waiting behind for him to go. 'By the way, the place is called Pachuka, and you need to take the boat to Lido . . .'

He pass me piece of paper with the Pachuka name on. Then they disappear with his sincere voice.

Lido? I know *Lido Holiday Inn Hotel*. It is the very expensive hotel in Beijing and Shanghai. Only foreigners live there, and Starbucks inside of those hotels in China. But, here, is the party also in *Lido*? Is it posh hotel too? Why I need take the boat to get there? Confused by all these thoughts, I walk alone to the waterbank, indecisive. Maybe I should go and pretend I am one of the famous Asian artists in the party. Westerners can't tell the difference of a group of Chinese. In their eyes, we all look the same. I decide ask someone the way to this *Lido*.

★   ★   ★

Taking the night boat, I am heading to the other side of Venice. I feel like living in the old time of south China, that people have to take boat to get to other places. I am staring at the water. Is this the sea? A real sea? I can't even see colour of water in the dark. It is very different the sea on pictures or in the film. It is also very different what you described me. I don't think anyone want swim in this water. Also, the sea is being stopped again and again by the city. How could be possible a city still stands here without sinking? I thought a sea is boundless. I am disappointed. I want tell you immediately how I'm feeling now. Chinese always say West culture is a blue culture, Chinese culture is yellow culture. This because West from the sea, and China comes from the yellow sand.

I don't understand the sea.

One hour later, I stand in front of 'Pachuka'.

From the outside it looks like a large restaurant or a night club. Neon lights everywhere. There are two very big men in the black suits, stopping everybody in front of the door. Some fashionable looking Italian mans and high-heel womans get in, with the invitation tickets holding in their hands. There are several India womans dressed up like queens or princess, also get into the door. It must be a really posh place, I wonder. I am glad I come here. But right now I can't remember that man's name. Gosh, why Western names are so difficult remember? So I wander around the door with my rocksack on shoulders and try to recall that name back. Antonia? Anthony? Andrew? Alexander? Antonioni? Which one sounds more closer?

Encouraging myself enormously, I walk to the door man: 'My friend asked me come here. He is inside.'

The door man answers in very rude and bad English: 'Sorry. It is a private party.'

'Yes, I know. But my friend invites me to come, and he is just inside the party,' I insist.

'What's your friend's name?'

'Antonia, Anthony, no, Andrew. Maybe Antonioni . . . You know I am a Chinese and I can't pronounce your country's name.' I am embarrassed myself.

'What does your friend do?'

'He is . . . he is the manager of the artists.' I just open my mouth randomly. I don't know him at all, and I don't think he is a manager of the artists.

One of the doormans takes it a little serious

221

and goes inside to ask somebody. One minute later he comes out:

'Sorry, we can't let you in.'

'But he invites me here. I should get inside!' I am pissed off.

'Sorry *Signorina*,' the door man says emotionlessly. 'No invitation, no entry. *Basta*.'

A posh car arrives, and three people come out with strange costumes and shining shoes. The bounce men say *Signori* to them, and they walk straight into the door. The music is loudly coming out from the party, and laughings. Nobody wants to take me in or even look at me a second. Why I don't look like one of the Asian artists? I wish I wear skirt, or some old-fashioned stupid traditional Chinese costumes.

I wander outside of the Pachuka like a wild night dog, no where to return. Then I see a very big and very long car arrives abruptly. Shit, it's a Cadillac! Comes out eight. Yes, one, two, three, four, five, six, seven, eight young womans. All blonde, with shining long golden hair. They wear the same miniskirt, and the same tight silver tops look just like bras. The silver miniskirts are so short people can see half of their bottoms. They are extremely slim, shapey, and all wear white high-heel long boots. They look like giraffes from the same giraffe mother. These sexy machines, leaded by a woman manager, their high-heels click the sandy ground: cha, cha, cha . . . They line up and one by one walking into the door. Two door mans fix their eyes on these girls body, like being deep frozen, can't move. What are these sex machines doing in this 'private party'?

Lap dancing? None of them are Asians. Or they will just drink champagne with posh mans guests?

I must have stayed in front of door nearly an hour watching all those fascinating guests. Then I see a taxi coming. And a man comes out from the taxi. That is him, the man I met two hours ago! Why did he arrive so late? Are Italian mans all like that?

'Antonia!' I shout.

Perhaps right name because he doesn't correct me, or maybe he didn't understand I am actually shouting his name.

He walks to me and apologise:

'I am very sorry about this. My friends changed their mind. They wanted to go somewhere else instead. In fact, it was better than this party. Let me take you to the other place.' His English accent is almost inunderstandable.

'All right.'

I don't want to tell him I wait here for so long. It would be not cool to let him know. So I follow him and get into his taxi.

Inside of taxi, so close, I can see his face clearly. He looks bit formal in his plain suit and black leather Made-in-Italy shoes. His hair is very few in the middle of his head. He seems sincerely but a little boring, if I can judge like that.

'So what you do?' I ask.

'I am an avocado,' he replies.

'Avocado?' I am surprised to hear. Is a fruit also a job? 'Please explain me,' I ask.

'If you are going to be put into prison, you can hire me to help you in the court,' he says.

'Ah . . . is like a lawyer?'

'Yes! Yes! Avocado is lawyer.' He is pleased that I understand.

'What about you?' he asks.

'I am . . . just a tourist. Actually I am studying English.'

'In Venice?' His interests are aroused.

'No. No. Studying English in England,' I say.

'Oh, your English is good.'

'Thank you. But why you are to do with this Asian culture festival?'

'Because of my friend, he is an avocado too. He gives legal advice to this organisation so he said, 'Andrea, come along too'.'

'I see.'

Gosh, not another avocado. At least now I know his correct name.

The taxi stops in front of a disco. Behind the disco is really the open sea. Is like a big pond full of black ink. I feel dangerous, as I think it's very easy to fall into that black pond.

It is a public disco, not 'private party'. It is already 2.30, the endless night. The music is so loud. American disco, it is too much for me. Lots of teenagers dancing inside. I want to leave immediately. But Andrea pull my arm into the dancing floor, and I see his friends are all there shaking their shoulders and tingling their heads. So we are dancing right in the middle of the floor, everyone tripping over my rocksack, and my head being hit heavily every single second by the crazy music. Oh, gosh, I can't dance like that, this is not my culture. My movements must be really ugly. It is a battle between the violent music and my boney body. And Andrea, he looks OK. He seems enjoying the music. His dancing style is a bit serious, but I am sure it better than mine.

I am getting so bored. So bored in the crowds. I can just stand there and fall in sleep like a horse.

'Are you OK?' Andrea dances towards me. His dancing almost like a slow walking.

'I am bit tired. Actually I want to go.' I say.

'Really? Where you stay?'

'I don't have a place to stay yet.'

'You don't? So where you are going to go now?' Andrea is talkative in the extremely loud music.

'I don't know.'

'Well, if you want, you can stay in my hotel. My room has two beds.'

'Really?'

'Yes, no problem.'

★ ★ ★

The taxi puts us in the middle of nowhere. Suburb, definitely suburb. There is a very simply looking hotel in front of us.

'Look, the sea is just over there.'

I look to where Andrea is pointing but there is only inky darkness.

'Do you see it?' he asks.

'Kind of,' I say.

He presses the door bell. Gosh, I feel

225

embarrassed. It is already half past four and if the hotel people know he brings a Chinese girl back, what they will think?

He presses the bell again.

'You know the man inside, his ears are not very good.' he explains.

'OK,' I comfort him.

Eventually there is a very old man opens the door. He even doesn't bother to raise his eyes to look. He says, '*Buona sera*' and then straight back to his room to sleep.

Andrea's room is in ground floor, just by main door of hotel. I am thinking tomorrow morning the reception will discover me easily and shame me.

He opens the room, and switches on the light. Then he shouts something like swear in Italian. He is scared.

'What is it?' I ask.

'There are some little animals here,' he shouts.

'Where?' I can't see anything.

'Here! Look the floor!' He points. There are some ants, big ants. They are moving around.

'Oh, just some ants.' I comfort him again and start put my feets on the ants, crush them with my shoes.

Andrea looks disturbed deeply. He runs into bathroom and pulls some toilet paper out. He kills rest of ants with paper, and flushes the paper into toilet.

There are two single beds. He didn't cheat me at all. I remove all my clothes, only left underwear. My pyjamas bottom of rocksack and don't want unpack. I cover myself tightly while he is in toilet brushing and flushing. Two minutes later he comes out and looks around for several seconds. He must be surprised to see how quick I am inside of the duvet. Then he asks:

'Should I turn off the light?'

'Yes. See you tomorrow,' I say.

In the darkness, I hear his snoring quickly comes. Honest snoring. I can tell. I am thinking he is quite a nice-heart man, but somehow he is not very interesting. Or maybe he is just normal. I count the hours to the morning. Two hours later it will be a sunny morning, and I will leave this damn island Lido and go to Venice . . .

I am almost fall sleep. Thinking of sex, no, I am having a dream about sex. Lesbian sex, me and a woman who has an unrecognisable face. Maybe she kisses me or touches my breast. Then I am suddenly awake. I feel somebody's lips press my lips. I open my eyes. Andrea is kissing me. He looks very stupid in the dim light.

'No. Go back to sleep,' I say. I feel a little disgust.

'OK,' he says obediently, then goes back to bed.

He looks funny. Wears a shorts but still with his white shirt. His two naked legs are a bit skinny and hairy.

I give up sleeping. I can sleep anytime in my forever Unlimited Inter-Rail train, so why waste time here in Lido? I get up and dress up. I brush my teeth and take all my belongs. Very quietly I close the door behind me.

The morning is never been so bright and fresh to me. The wind is blowing my yellow skin. I feel free. I feel my body is entirely free. I walk to the seashore. There are some little boats are swinging on the sea. The sea is truly blue. Pure blue like a dream. The water is like a magnet, attracting my body towards it. I agree with you, sea is beautiful.

'I feel sad about my life,' you once said to me.
'Why?'
'Everything feels empty and endless.'
'What you want then?'
'I want to find happiness.'
'You can't have happiness at all times. Sometimes you will be sad. Don't you think?'
'But I don't see any happiness in my life.'
'Then what's your most near happiness?'
' . . . The sea.'

That was our conversation one day, in our home in London. Now it is like a replay. It echoes above the waves.

tavira

A very slow and old train, clink, clink, clink . . . it is so slow that it's like I am sitting on a real time machine. I can feel the time moving in the space physically. It is much more interesting than watching clock.

The train moves along the south coast of Portugal. I didn't stay in Madrid or anywhere in Spain because I lost eighty euros when train stopped in Madrid. Maybe they are being stolen. I didn't feel like to stay in the big city anymore. It is always aggressive in the city. Here, the train patiently takes me to Tavira, a little town close to Atlantic Ocean, yellow sand everywhere.

Out of the station I find blocks of old

residential houses, decayed in the hot sun. I walk to a corner café between two streets, white plastic tables and white chairs outside. I sit down, breathe out, get rid of the stale and take in the fresh. Suddenly I feel everything slow down and stop. In the shade of sun, two old local mans with very dark skin sit on the chair. They are smoking, quiet, in the morning. Two little tiny coffee cups are left empty in front of them. Everything is brewing very thick in the early morning here, like the sun, with passionate beams. They got a real sun here in their sky, not like in England. English sun is a fake sun, a literature sun.

The other side of the café is a grocery shop. Some vegetables and fruits are being sold. A young woman standing outside, she seems mad, I mean, real mad. She keeps talking to nobody, and there is no anybody there at all, not even a wild dog. She wears fleshly red lipsticks like she just drank a glass of blood. Sometimes a car passes by and she talks to the car. Strange, somehow there is always a mad woman in any little town in the world.

A young girl, looks like a backpacker, a tourist, wanders in the street. She wears a tight lemon-colour T-shirt. Her young lively breasts drag those old local man's eyes. As she disappears into the end of the street, two old mans withdraw back their eyes, and both exhale the smoke from their mouths. It must be a pleasure for them, in the morning street, seeing a young active breast under the lemon T-shirt.

The sunlight is like a knife cutting off the

earth, half of the world is in the shadow, and the other half is bright. It is like a black and white movie, and everything is in slow motion. The sky is deadly blue, blue and blue. In alley ways, the old houses are silent, with rusty iron balcony and wooden window. They are sucking people's soul. I understand why some foreigners travelled to a strange town for a short stay, but one month passed by, and then three months passed by, still there, and eventually ended up to live there for the rest of their life. That strange power, forces a person settle down a foreign land, whatever how wild he was. I can feel that strange power. It is something opposite of adventure, something comes from the living habits, and acceptance of monotonous, the monotonous of everyday's life.

Sitting in this corner café with old mans, I am melted under the hot sun. My body is losing its shape, and floating in the air. My entirely existence is being sucked by a strange power. It scares me.

★　★　★

I find room on top floor of Residencia Mina. A budget hotel. The room is narrow but clean. With the beautiful sky light it feels light hearted. I love this small Mediterranean-style hotel. Standing on balcony I can see the river wriggle and connect to the sea. The sand is dark yellow, and the houses are colourful. Two or three old mans sit on the bridge above the river, smoking, chatting. The old streets, the green bushes, the sea birds . . . All these are exposed under the sun. I feel very close to the nature, the happy side of the nature.

I climb the steps up to roof of hotel. It is like a tropical garden, full of pot-planted palm trees and flowers. The sea not far away, shining in the distance. There are several ferries carry people to the outskirt part of beach. It is high noon, and the late summer sun is really hot. I take off my shirt, letting my body naked. It feel so good I take off the rest of my clothes. My soul is dancing. If happiness is a brief matter, then I am in this brief moment. I wonder whether the sadness inside a human sometimes is just because of lack of sunlight.

I think of you, while I am naked lying on the roof garden. We used to make love so often in your garden, by the fig tree. I remember all those details of when we were making love. I remember that you would take out my earrings before we make love. I remember that they were always entwined in my hair, very difficult to come out, but you would try hard to remove. That is you. That is one of the details I will always remember about you.

Unconsciously, I touch my earrings, but they are not there now. I am getting restless. I feel my nipples getting hard. I want to be exposed and touched in the hot sunlight. I think of book I bought in the train station while I was bored waiting:

Women's Pleasure or How To Have An Orgasm As Often As You Want

Question: 'How do I build up my skills?'

There are two ways in which you build up your masturbation skills:

1) By doing it more frequently.

2) By doing it in a variety of different situations. This creates the sexual versatility that is so important to your progress.

Below are fifteen different ways of masturbating that you can practise. These fifteen methods are divided into four lessons.

Lesson 1: Masturbation in private
Lesson 2: Masturbation in semi-public
Lesson 3: Masturbation in public
Lesson 4: Improving your timing

Masturbating, I never tried it before. Nobody Western would believe that I never try to masturbate as a twenty-four-year-old woman. Or maybe I did but I didn't know what I was doing. Sex in my understanding means something to do with a man, but not to do with myself. Having sex with oneself is like talking to oneself: bit mad. When I saw that Soho peepshop, I never thought to do with me. I also believed no love then no sex. Sex is an expression of love. But somehow this idea is changing. Now I feel tortured by the desire inside my body, and I feel strongly how much this desire wanting to be fulfilled.

'You should learn to play with your own clitoris.' Once you told me this on the bed. We were naked, and we had just made love.

233

Your hand touched my body. 'If you want to have an orgasm, you should touch yourself here.'

I remember this conversation. But I never did it with myself, because I was always with you. Why do I have to?

On the roof of Residencia Mina, through the trees, the sun penetrates my skin. The leaves rustle in the mild wind. I start to touch myself.

The juice flows from my cave, and my fingers touch my hidden lips. Up and down. A great urge coming over me like a high tide flooding my body. The only thing I can see is the blue sky. The deep blue, like a boundless sea. The dry leaves under my skin are wet from my desire.

My body starts to shake. My breath gets difficult. My cave wants to devour something. I want to shout. It is almost painful, I feel like crying.

And I scream.

On my own. With myself. I did it. It is like dream.

For the first time in my entire life, I came by myself.

I can be on my own. I can. I can rely on myself, without depending on a man.

faro

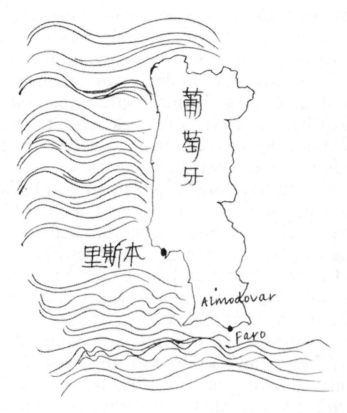

The train from Faro to Lisbon will depart at 1.30 in the afternoon. It's twelve o'clock now. I learned Faro is a *resort* town. From the dictionary the *resort* place must be a very nice place, but in reality it is the opposite. Faro is very concrete. Almost ugly. What should I do in little *resort* to kill one and half an hour?

I walk around the train station with my rocksack on my back. The sea is just by the train station. But this sea smells bad. Between the sea and the inner land is an industry space, no beach. The rocks nearby the shore are dirty, polluted. It smells pee or something unpleasant. But some seagulls still convolute there. I feel sorry for those seagulls. I walk back to the street nearby the train station. People sitting outside of cafés looks at me. I can feel their curiosity to me. I bet there is few Chinese people come to this town. What is like looking this Chinese girl through their eyes? Without a companion with her, lost herself in the street, doesn't know what to do about her life . . . Or maybe they just think of Chinese food when they see me.

12.30, still have one hour left to go to Lisbon. I sit outside of a café, having a small cup of bitter espresso. How many cups of espresso the Portuguese have in one day? What is like if one's body full of caffeine and sugar and nicotine and Coca Cola? Will it bring too much passion? Will the life be more energetic?

The espresso cup is dried up. I start to read *Lonely Planet* on Lisbon with my small *Concise* dictionary. The man in the nearby table is drinking the second cup of espresso. I am aware his watching on me. He is lighting a cigarettes now. He looks at the street, and then the blue sky, and me again. Now he stands and comes to me, and he sits on the chair very near to me.

He says: 'Can you understand it?'

'Understand what?'

I close my guide book and look at him. He seems a very physical person, maybe he does low jobs. But he can speak good English. He is short, dark, energetic, solid strong body, broad chest, impressive face, intensive brown eyes.

236

'Understand the language. Because you are checking the dictionary all the time.'

Inside of his mouth, something strange. Some teeth missing there.

'Well, you know, I am a foreigner.' I am a little embarrassed.

'Don't read the book. Look at the view. You should see it, not read the guide book.' He surveys my books. There is Fernando Pessoa's *Book of Disquiet* lies on top.

'OK,' I say. He is definitely from local. I wonder if he reads Fernando Pessoa. He looks like a person doesn't read any book at all.

'How many days you are going to stay in Faro?' he asks.

'Not anymore. I just came here for taking train to Lisbon, in one hour.'

By hearing this, he has no comments. There are no needs to develop more connection from his side, I guess.

'Do you know where is the old town of Faro? Do you think I can have time to walk there in one hour and come back?' I ask.

'Not very far. If you want I can take you to there.'

'Don't you have anything to do?'

'Not today. Come with me.' He stands up and goes to pay the bill. I stand up as well, put my books in my bag.

As I follow him, I look his back. A very physical manly back. A little short. A very earthy person. I wonder if he works in a local restaurant, or works on a wine factory, or maybe he is a sailor, a carpenter, a trolley driver . . .

The old town of Faro is nothing very special, except for the old slipperly cobblestone ground. I like these cobblestones, they were being grind so smooth by thousands of millions people's foot through centuries. They got stories in them. Then we walk into an old square. This man wants to show me the church. But the old church is closed today, so does the museum. Do people not working here in the afternoon time? Only a small souvenir shop opened, selling some postcards about Faro in the nineteenth century. The middle-day sunlight is strong. We want buy ice cokes from that souvenir shop. He only pays his coke, I notice. Of course, it is fair for him.

We drink ice coke, wander on the empty cobblestone square.

'I'll take you to the seaside, then you can go back to the train station.' He walks beside me.

'I already went there. It is not very beautiful.' I want to be honest.

'No, believe me. I'll take you to a nice place.'

'OK.'

He takes my heavy rocksack, and puts it on his back.

We walk along the seashore beside the railway. A marsh is just in front of us. It is muddy, and dirty. The marsh reflects the high noon's sunlight. It looks bizarre and dangerous. There is something very strange between him and me. He is almost too kind, too random, without any goal in his daily life. At the same time he is also very sexual. I don't know where this sexual feeling exactly from, maybe from his very physical looking. Or maybe this sexual feeling from myself, from my aloneness. My body is waiting for something, and something has to come out under the intensive sun.

He takes my hand, and I don't refuse at all. I don't know why. He holds my hand into his hand so tight that in one minute our palms are sweaty. I could feel there is something strong inside of his body. But I am not sure if I enjoy this *intimacy*. I am a bit confused. We walk side by side like two longterm friends. I know I don't love him at all, and maybe I even don't like him, but somehow I desire him. It is strange.

Maybe the more people live close to the south, the more they are talkative. They have to take out the extra energy inside of their bodies from the sun. Now he is doing a monologue:

'I don't like Faro, you know. It is not as nice as other places in Portugal. It is full of English people. Food is expensive, and everything is for tourists. But why I am here? Why I am sitting here doing nothing? Because I lost my four teeth, six years ago. Four! Can you see here? A motorbike accident. A big accident. I had three motorbikes before, you know. But not anymore, since I sold them all. I am not going to touch motorbikes anymore. I would die if I ride motorbike again. I have been waiting for the medical insurance to fix my teeth for six years. Six years! Can you believe it? Bastards! Things are so slow in this country! Papers and papers. Finally it is arranged. That's why I came back here, to get my teeth done. I worked in Germany. Look up here, can you see here? These two teeth? They'll take out these two from the upper jaw, and I am going to have my new teeth, six new teeth.'

I look at his teeth again, with my new eyes. It is really impressive. How a person left the mouth so empty?! Does his tongue feel cold?

'But why you were in Germany?' I ask.

'I worked in Germany, you know, in Cologne. I was a chef. You know what a chef is, don't you? I cooked for people. Cologne is a good place, yes, the people are friendly there. I earned good money in Cologne. You know, the economy is no good in this country, only the weather is good here . . . '

Our hands still hold together. We stop under a palm tree. Some empty coke tins, empty crisps bags spread around the tree. There are rocks by our feet, but covered by the dead small fish and dry weeds. So much polluted, it smells horrible. He leads me against the tree, and hugs me, and kisses my neck. Then kisses my ears. His lips are hot. And his tongue is strong, almost violent. I don't refuse him. Maybe I also want it. Then he touches my breasts. He presses his palm on my lower body. His breathing becomes strong and heavy. I hug him too. And I can feel his heart beating fast. The sun, the sweat, the salty wind, the stinking air, everything is stimulating our desires.

I say: 'I think I want to have sex with you.'

This man takes what I said. And everything comes rapidly and naturally. Finding a piece of flat rock, I unzip my jeans, and I sit on top of that piece of hot rock, with my naked crotch. He

240

kneels down and he buries himself between my legs. It is so wet, everything is so wet, my crotch, his tongue, his sweaty skin, and my striped underwear. It is like the tide, a strong tide comes taking people away from the beach. His hands reach his jeans, and untie the button at the same time.

'But no plugging in. Please.' I don't know how to say that. And I am suddenly scared by what we are doing: 'No. I don't want that. Just using sucking me. Please, please,' I beg him.

I just realise I don't want he enter into my body. No. It would disgust me so much.

But he couldn't control himself anymore. He takes out his penis from his jeans and pushes it into my body, rough, almost violent.

I am leaning on the rock. I feel sexy but I also feel disgusting at the same time. The sunlight makes me headache. I can't breathe. Somehow I despise him doing that. Then he comes. He comes like a bull. He pulls out, the sperm dripping on the burning rocks. His face is completely red.

I will never trust this man again I tell myself. Nothing will be between him and me anymore. Not anymore, I swear to myself. I feel a strong guilt, and danger. I despise myself.

We put on clothes, and the dirty feeling of my body is overwhelming. It sticks on my skin, my underwears, my jeans, and my white T-shirt. It is under my skin. And the sea seems even dirtier and even more polluted than before. Empty plastic bottles half buried in the sand. Black plastic bags floating on the foaming sea water. I just want to leave this place, leave him, as quick as possible.

★ ★ ★

The train is ready to leave. He is standing behind me in the train station café. I want to buy some water, and I want to find a place like a toilet can wash myself. I can't stand the dirt on my skin, and I can't stand the strange smell from his body. His clothes smells of strong perfume. I can't stand it for one more second. It makes me vomit. But as the train approaches into the sight in the distance, he suddenly says:

'Something very bad happened.'

'What?'

'Look here.' He turns around and shows me the back pocket of his jeans. There is a hole underneath the pocket.

'I just lost fifty euros,' he says, with a worried tone.

I look at him. His face is covered by emptiness and vagueness. I think of what he just said. He was quite cool before, or say half an hour ago. Now he becomes very weak, suddenly. When I met him, I thought he was just a normal local man having espresso in a café. I thought he was just as simple and happy as the weather in Portugal. But now I don't know what to feel anymore.

'Now I can't even buy a bus ticket to go back home,' he says. His hand is still on his pocket with a hole.

The train arrives and the door is opened.

242

What should I say about that hole? What should I do about this strange fifty euros? No, don't start to think. Don't start to talk about it. Just leave this topic. Don't ask, don't say anything more. I take my rocksack from his shoulders, and I walk to the platform without hesitation.

'Bye,' I say, with a cold smile.

I step on the train. Don't look back. Don't look back now. The door is closed behind me, thanks God. And that's it.

I walk straight to the toilet on the train. I unload my bags on the floor of toilet. I remove my clothes, my jeans, my pants. And I turn on the tap. I wash myself completely.

dublin

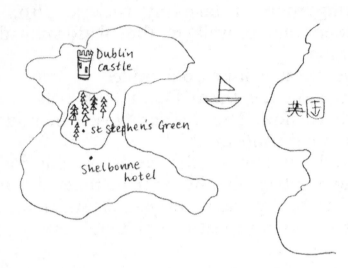

Dublin, my last stop. I flew Dublin. I am not in Continent anymore.

This is the most western place I ever been in my life. I never been to States, and anway I don't know if States is more west than Europe since the earth is round. When I was in China, I thought Dublin is in the middle of Berlin, because that's how Chinese translated the word 'Dublin'. Also I thought London in the middle of the whole Europe, because Britain sounds so big: 'the empire on which the sun will never set'. So London must be in the centre Europe just like Chinese character for China, '中国', it means a country in the centre of the world.

I have some difficulties from the start — I am being stopped at the customs in the Dublin airport.

'Do you have a visa?' the immigration officer sitting in the glass box asks me seriously.

Is he blind or something? Can he not see those important stamps on my passport? I stare at him, with big confidence: 'Of course I have visa.'

'Where is it?' He throws my passport on the table.

I am a bit annoyed by this Westerner. I grab my passport back and open page where I got Schengen Visa stamp.

'Here it is!' I point the visa to the blind man. 'Can't you see it is a Schengen visa?'

'But we are not in a Schengen country,' says the man in very sober voice.

I am confused: 'But I was told that your Irish use euros, just like in France, or Germany!'

'That doesn't mean we are a Schengen country. You need a visa to come into this country.'

For one moment I really scared. Then I remember my UK visa. Quickly I find page where I have my student visa stamp from UK Embassy. I am so clever.

The man looks at the visa one second only and says, 'We are not part of the British Empire either.'

He throws my passport on the table again.

I stare at that officer and don't know what to do. Will they send me back to the UK? Or will they send me back to China, straight away? I don't have return ticket. If now they send me back, will I need to pay the air tickets? Or will they pay the fee?

I am standing in the corner of the Customs, all

the passengers passed by, and new passengers from some other strange countries all left too. I am remained alone. After a while, I see the officer gives my passport to a new officer, then he leaves. This new officer is a very kind man, probably he is from less-west-country. He lets me fill a form, then he checks through the form. And then he lets me stand in front of the camera. Gosh, I never notice there is a camera underneath the glass box of the customs! I stand there and try to smile and being innocent. The nice man says OK, and he stamps on my passport.

'What is that stamp?' I am so worried that he stamps something terrible, terrible for my future.

'It means next time, if you come to Ireland without a visa, you will be illegal.' He gives me back the passport with a black stamp allowing me short-period stay provided no working.

'Do you understand?' the officer asks.

'Yes. Yes. Thanks you.'

I hold the passport like holding rest of my life.

★   ★   ★

Walking around Dublin I lost myself again. I am wandering in a park — St Stephen's Green. There is a lake in the park, and some swans live there. There are also some weird birds with green neck swimming on the water. The rain arrives, it is like rain curtain. It rains intensely. Nobody, no any plants, no any single leafs, can avoid the madness of the rain. I run out of the park. By

246

the park, there is a hotel called The Shelbourne Hotel. I walk in.

The hotel is marvellous. Somebody plays piano in the lobby. There is a fireplace, or no, two in the ground lobby. The fire is burning. I stare at the fire. I love watching fire, better than TV — the way it changes the shape all the time. The burning things inside are not like coal, or charcoal, or wood. It is a kind of black, long square piece of bar. I never see that before. I sit down on the old-soft-posh-arm-chaired sofa and feel the fire sucks my wetness from the rain.

'Excuse me, do you know what is this stuff burning in the fire?' I ask an old gentleman on next sofa. He is in black bowler hat and dark coat, with his tall black umbrella. He is like from Sherlock Holmes story, an old detective.

'I beg your pardon?' the old man says.

'You know this stuff, the stuff is burning, what do you call that?' I point to the fireplace.

'Ah, those are *briquettes*, my dear,' the old man answers proudly.

'Briquettes?' Why it sounds like a French bread?

'We also call it peat, my dear,' the old man adds, 'or turf.'

The old man look at my deeply confused face. He gets up to perform for me, to help me to understand: 'In the old times we in Ireland used spades to cut the turf. Then we'd dry it.' He is doing the gesture of digging and chopping.

The old man has very strong accent, and my English listening comprehension becomes hopeless.

'Turf' Or 'Tofu'? I don't understand this word. Gosh, why they don't simply call it 'black burning stuffs'?

A young handsome waiter comes with a menu.

'Would you like to order something?' the waiter asks politely.

'Yes, sure.' Of course, I have to pretend somebody posh from Japan or Singapore. I shall leave here as soon as my clothes are dried up.

The waiter gives me a big book of menu.

The old man pays the bill. He takes his tall-huge-old umbrella and salute with his black bowler hat to me: 'Good bye, young lady.'

★　★　★

Five days in Ireland, I am lying on bed inside of youth hostel just reading *Intimacy*. Sometimes I look up in the dictionary, but the more I read, the less I care the new words like *Thatcherites* and *Terpsichorean*. I don't care what they mean. I understand the whole story completely anyway without dictionary. In that book, what the man wants from his wife is the intimacy, but his wife doesn't give it to him. So he leaves for a new lover, for a new, passionate life. Don't you know that all I want is be *intimate* with you?

In Dublin, that morning I finish reading the last page of the book, I decide go back London as quickly as possible. I am tired of travel. I am longing to see you.

I quickly pack my bag in the youth hostel and I walk out of this place where full of loud university students and hippies. Perhaps these people don't need intimacy, or they have got it enough, or it worth nothing to them while they listen i-pod and dance in the clubs all night long.

October

self

self n distinct individuality or identity of a person or thing; one's basic nature; one's own welfare or interests

The plane touches down at London Stansted airport. It is afternoon. Outside is raining, dim as usual. I am standing by the luggage belt, waiting for my rocksack. Has it gone to Los Angeles or Delhi or something? Everybody took their luggages but mine doesn't come. Almost an hour later, last person took his suitcase from the belt.

I go to the 'Lost Luggage' counter to report. A man apologises to me and says he will find out and contact me. Luckily, I have my passport with me.

You are not waiting meet me so I take train to home. I have nothing to bring back from my travel. I lost my *Dubliners*, lost my Fernando Pessoa, lost *Intimacy*. I also lost all the maps you gave to me. And I lost my toothbrush, lost my clothes and lost my address book. I only have the stories that happened in an East Berlin flat, in Amsterdam under the wisteria tree, on the Lido in Venice, in Faro . . . They stay in my heart and my skin.

London evening: everything comes back to me

quickly. The slow and noisy tube, the oily fish and chip shop, the dim and crowded pubs, the raining streets with people waiting for their never-coming bus. London is such a desolate place.

The house is empty. But everywhere smells of you. And there is much mess. All your tools are on the floor. And your bags of clay and plaster are piled up in the living room. In the kitchen I find a line of dirty tea cups on the table and there is a sculputure of a bath, made from plastic, lying in the middle of the floor. It is making joke of me. Only the plants are living quietly in the garden. The fruit tree without flower stands there, still holding the peace of the garden. There are yellow leafs everywhere covering your sculptures. I pick up one fig. It is almost rotten and the juice immediately comes out. I taste it, very sweet. The seeds are sandy in my mouth. In these five weeks I am absent, nature changed so much. Every plant has a different shape. And you? In these five weeks, has anything changed on you?

I turn on the radio. Weather report, as important as yesterday and tomorrow. A man talks with a very low tone like he just knew England lost football match:

'The rest of today will be overcast, with rain predicted for much of the weekend. There's a small chance of occasional sunshine so let's keep our fingers crossed . . . '

Yes. Let's keep our fingers crossed.

I wash all the tea cups, and all the dirty plates. I sweep the floor, and I let your sculptures lean

254

against the wall. I put all your socks and smelly shirts into the washing machine. I tidy your table. Then I sit and I wait.

When the last beam of light in the sky has disappeared, you come back home with a bunch of your friends. You hug me, say hello to me, just like you would hug and hello another friend. Then everybody sits down, smoking cigarettes, having tea, talking English jokes, and laughing loudly. I never could understand jokes. And I know you hate smokers, but now you let your friends smoke everywhere in the house. *Friendship*. A respectful term.

I try to join in the conversation, but it is frustrating.

Your friends are talking about transsexual surgery, turning a person from male to female. One woman has very heavy make-up and long blonde curly hair. But there's something strange about her, she somehow looks very manly. Probably she was a man before. Gosh, how do I know.

She is an expert:

'Is he sure about it? I tell you, darling, if he really wants to do it, then he should get it done in the States. I can give him all the contacts, and a breakdown of the costs.'

'So, how much does it work out at?' one of your friends is eager to know.

'Well, Dr Brownstein's fee is about $7,750, and the Surgical Facility fee is around $3,000 ... but then there's a whole list of other shit — the Anaesthesia costs $700 ... '

'Bloody hell!' the eager one says.

255

'So, tell us a bit more about the surgery,' another asks.

'Well, it's a pretty complicated process. The doctor has to create a vagina, and work out the maximal clitoral and vaginal sensation, but minimising scars . . . '

I am chopping some carrots and try to follow the conversation. The carrots are so hard.

I listen, and listen, and listen carefully, I even stop chopping carrots. But in the end I am lost. I am an outsider. And nobody can deny this. I am just somebody's peasant wife. I feel lonely. I just want to talk to you, without the others here. I feel like all the expectation I collected on the journey is going to nowhere. I am getting bitter. I doubt if my absence of five weeks in this house affect you at all.

While they carry on their intense conversation about transsexual, I tell you that I lost my rocksack. And I lost all your maps. You say never mind, you don't need those maps anymore.

One of your friends heard I just came back from Europe.

'So you went to Dublin?'

'Yes.'

'How was it?'

'It was good.'

Another person says:

'How was Paris?'

'Paris was good,' I answer.

The third person asks:

'Did you like Venice?'

'Yes, I did.'

'That's good,' she replies.

256

Is that how English people speak? If so, then I must be a bit English now.

Eventually all your friends leave. Only the trails of smoke drift around the ceiling, and empty glasses stay on the table. Here we are, face to face, only two of us.

You put the kettle on, and sit down towards me.

'So, how are you my darling? Do you want a cup of tea?'

'No.'

'Are you sure?'

'Yes. If you want some then you have some. I don't want any.'

'OK.' You look at me, and observe the mood on my face.

'You love lots of people, but I only love you.' I speak, painfully. I just want to push the subject right to the front line.

'What's the problem now? Don't you think I love you?'

'I don't feel that intimacy with you like before.'

'Why not?'

'I don't know. It feels like you don't really need me, and you never really needed me. I don't know why I came back here.'

'What do you mean? Nothing has changed. I'm the same person as before.'

'But I feel you are cold. We haven't made love for such a long time but you didn't even kiss me when you walked through the door. I missed you so much, I wrote you emails everyday as possible as I can, but how many emails did you write to me in the last whole month? Only five! You knew

I would be back tonight but you still brought your friends. Didn't you want to be with your lover *privately*? Are your friends more important than your lover?'

I am so angry. I can see my anger everywhere in the house.

'Of course I love you. But that doesn't mean I have to abandon my friends. I think you are being a bit selfish,' you say.

'Thank you! Yes, I am a very *selfish* person. I am so selfish that I want to have a quiet night with my lover after five weeks travel!'

I try hold my anger back. I don't know what I can say. I know you didn't have sex with anybody when I was away, and I am the one did all these messy things. How can I blame you? But at the same time I feel so disappointed about you.

'I don't think I am a special one to you at all,' I shout.

I walk into the bathroom. I turn on the bath. I take off my clothes. And I clean myself away from all those dusts.

The night when our bodies lie down side by side, I feel I am detached. We are not one body anymore. This is the first time I feel this. There is a big obsessed 'self' separating itself from my body and looking at your body. Even when we make love, even when your body is deeply in my body . . .

★   ★   ★

We Chinese are not encouraged to use the word 'self' so often. The old comrades in the work unit would say, how can you think of 'self' most of the time but not about others and the whole society?

The 'self' is against 'group' and 'collectivism'. The 'self' is the enemy of the Communist party. In middle school we were taught 'the most admirable person' should forget about himself, shouldn't satisfy his own needs.

I remember in my middle school whole class went to the Old People's House every Friday afternoon. It was a big place for old lonely people to stay, but also abandoned babies were being raised there. The babies were always girls, girls who had been found in the rubbish bin or in the street. I remember there were lots of tiny babies sleeping in one room. We brought our soaps and basins from home, to wash the nappies and clothes. I remember several baby girls have strange white spotted skin and white hair. We were frightened to see that. We were told these babies had a special skin disease. We were scared to touch them in case our body turned to white too. And I remember two babies with strange shapes of the body. Their fingers were bound together, one of the legs twisted like vines. I was horrified. But it taught us to understand other mankind's miseries and sufferings; to understand how lucky we are compare with these hopeless people.

But here, in this rainy old capitalism country, 'self' means everything, 'self' is the original creativity for everything. Art, business, fashion, society system, all deeply depend on this 'self'. The connection between the world and 'self' is so strong. 'Self' works incredibly well.

259

abortion

abortion n operation to end a pregnancy; *Informal* something grotesque

My period still didn't come. I wait one week. Then two. Not a single drop of blood. In a vague afternoon, I decide to go to the pharmacy buy a pregnancy test box. I come back home and you are not here. I shall find out on my own. The blue symbol shows a cross: positive.

Holding the pregnant test sample in my hand, I don't know if this baby is from you. I really don't know. I look at that cross again and my body feels so dirty. I want to wash myself.

I wait the whole day for you to come back home. When you come back in the evening, I tell you. I say I need to go to hospital and have an abortion. As quick as possible. Surprisingly, you don't say anything. You don't even ask when it happened, and you don't even ask if it is from you. You just look at me with sad face and I start to cry. You put your arms around me and hold me tight.

Five days later you drive me to a clinic in Richmond, with your broken white van. We stop in a petrol station. Is it very far away? I ask. Not very far, you answer, we will get there soon. Your van is old but it is never really totally broken down. Highway. So many cars. So many traffic lights. I feel dizzy. Everything goes fuzzy. I don't know what you are thinking about this baby might be yours. All I know is you hold my hand very tight, only let go change gear. I feel you are only stable thing to me. You are my life.

⋆　⋆　⋆

I wake up on a wheel bed, without feeling anything unusual. I eat the orange and biscuits the nurse gives to me. I put on my coat and find my shoes back. No more fear anymore, only the sorrow of emptiness. I walk slowly back to the resting room. I see you. You stand up from piles of newspaper, walk towards me.

Going to van, your hand is under my waist, and I am feeling weak. We look like other typical couple who just lost their baby. When we push the garden gate in front of the clinic, somebody stops us. A little old lady in black is like a ghost standing in front of us. Her hair is grey and wrinkles cover her face. She is skinny like a skeleton, and I can see her bones and her blood vessels through her skins. She gives me little piece of card from a plastic bag, then she quickly disappears in the street. On the card there are three lines of printing:

> INDEPENDENT FAMILY PLANNING ADVICE.
> WE ARE HERE TO HELP YOU AND YOUR
> UNBORN CHILD.
> CONFIDENTIAL.

On back is a telephone number and an address. But it is too late.

No, my dear little old lady, we wanted abortion. I wanted to do abortion. Everybody comes to this clinic for the same thing. Has this lady seen how many single womans there are in the resting room inside the clinic, sitting there waiting for hours because they want to have an abortion?

I begin to feel much better after we leave the clinic. I feel my body going back to normal. I can feel my hormone levels return to normal. I feel relieved.

nostalgia

nostalgia n sentimental longing for the past

'You need nourishment,' you say to me.

So you buy lots of food for me from Tescos. The baby is gone so I shall eat a lot to fill the emptiness. Salad, shrimp, fried chickens ... Everything on the back of the package is '*Produced for Tesco Stores Ltd*'. In my hometown, when a woman has abortion, her mother cooks eel ginger soup, or a soup made from dates and lotus seeds. But not here. Here, Tesco packages look after you.

You are cooking some obscure pie for me. It is called q-u-i-c-h-e. I have never seen it before. On the bag it says:

Even Real Men Eat Quiche!

Quiche, q-u-i-c-h-e. I can't believe it when I am swallowing this piece of shapeless hot stuff. Such an ambiguous piece of food. Totally formless. I wonder about what my parents would say if one day they come to this country, and they eat this. My mother probably will say: 'It is like eating something from other people's mouth.' And my father will say: 'It must be left from earlier meal so they re-cook it but inside are already messed up.'

I will agree with my father: it is a piece of big mess indeed. You tell me it is actually from France. I don't believe you. I think the English are too ashamed to acknowledge it is their food. So they say it is French to defend themself.

But, in the evening, you cook a fish for me. Not cod, not seabass, not any typical English fish. It is a silver carp. It is like my hometown's fish. It smells of the river nearby our house. I remember I studied a word before, and I remember how to pronounce this word. No-stal-gia. Eating carp causes my *nostalgia*.

age

age n length of time a person or thing has existed; time of life; latter part of human life; period of history; long time

Today when you unload some box from your van, you become extremely tired. You become really old. We used to look like five years difference in other people's eye, but now obvious twenty years gap between us. This makes me feel a little sad about you. You look at me, a small smile. There is a shadow underneath your eyes. Maybe it is me made you old. I not go out earn live. And I always demand love from you. I demand love by showing my vulnerability, again and again. I remember at the beginning of us, you have a perfect hair. But now, there is a bit grey hidden behind your ears. And your wrinkles, they are at the corner of your eyes. Sometimes I wonder if you saw these wrinkles, if you saw your grey hair hidden behind your ears.

You used to believe in totally individual life, no family, no marriage. You used to think that a personality could never be change. But recently you said, 'People do change, they always change.' Look at now. You are forced by my vulnerable to show a solid love to me, to show a practical love to me. Since abortion you try hard to keep a family with me, by doing the practical things. You are tired, physically, and maybe spiritually as well.

Is this the love I want from you? Maybe I always want you become old, always want your charm in front of others disappear. So you would be weaker. Then we could be *equal*.

I walk towards to your van, and I help you to move the boxes which are full of bottles of wines. These boxes will be delivered to some shops in two days. The box is heavy. You will not leave in the van, because gangs in Hackney smashed your van and tried to steal whatever they could steal. You can't trust people here, you said. We carry the box into kitchen, and put on ground, carefully and slowly.

'Why you have to do this kind of job? Why don't you try hard sell your sculptures?' I ask. 'Why you need always more money? You own your house. Is that not enough?' I continue. 'If big problem, we can just move to China where your West money make you rich.'

'Listen, why can't you just shut up for once and let me do my own thing,' you say.

I hate myself being so needy. The way I want of love, is like a hard toothbrush try to brush bad teeth, then it ends up bleeding. The harder I try, more blood comes out. But I believe love can cure everything, and eventually the teeth will not bleeding anymore. I still think love is the hope, of everything.

'*Just the two of us, we can make it if we try. Just the two of us, building castles in the sky. Just the two of us, you and I . . .*'

The music is very loud comes out from neighbour's window.

lighthouse

lighthouse n tower with a light to guide ships

The train takes us to Wales. It is our first holiday
together. It feels fresh. We should have done this
long ago, we should have done this before we
started fighting, before everything fell apart.
Now I know why there are so many holidays in
the West.

It was your idea to come to this place. You
want to leave city, you want your lungs to inhale
the air from the mountains and the sea. And I
agree. I agree because I think travelling together
may help us, may remove the illness in our
relationship.

In the windy afternoon, we arrive at west
Wales. Coming out from the train, I breathe out
the filth from London. The Irish Sea is
underneath the mountain. The sky is high, and
the trees are dark green. People in Wales walk
slower than in London. They move slowly, drive
slowly, laugh slowly, they spend time slowly. You
said to me, ancient people believed humans
would lose their soul if they walked too fast. So
people here must have strong soul.

The mountain climbs up from some huge
rocks. Piles and piles of black rocks tumble down
to the sea. We walk from the valley to the

mountain. The mountain is enormous. It is continually connected to another mountain, and another mountain behind. So high, it is close to the heaven. The cliffs are steep, without any plants. Perhaps the wind too strong for plants growing. Such a bleak landscape, there seems no hesitation, no confusion. When we walk on the mountain, we see the grass grows short and hard, rooted into the soil like needles. And the soil underneath my feet is very hard too. Climbing, climbing, I can hear my breath and yours, heavy and strong.

We walk into the bushes, the yin side of the mountain. It is dark and muddy. Roots are everywhere underneath my feet. We walk into the forest. The forest is decaying, wet and lush. The world becomes even quieter. You are loving it. Your body becomes lively, and you look like a man in his twenties. The birds are singing on branches, and leafs brush against each other in the wind. We sit down, inhaling and exhaling. You pick up chestnut case beside you. Green case is old, brown and sad. But when you open it, inside is silky and smooth and gentle. It smells of spring.

I see your love towards that chestnut, and I can feel my love to you.

The dark clouds quickly cover the sky, and the early evening of the winter arrives. There is something unknown hidden in the forest. There is something sucking the human soul. And I feel like soon we will be swallowed by the nature. I find the beauty of the nature can be a terror, but I don't know if you feel the same way.

We stay in a B&B, a very old stone house. It is a village in Pembrokeshire, a village on the mountain, a village buried in green weeds, a village hidden in the night fogs, a village which have the sky holds the stars and the moon.

I lose sleep during the night. It is raining all the time. Since we arrived here I haven't slept for one second. I think it is because I can't get used to the quietness here. The quietness is so strong that it is almost unbearable noisy. It is so quiet everywhere that I hear all kinds of noises. I even can hear moss growing.

While I am lying on the bed with you, in this strange stone house at night, I know the rain is covering the woods, and the sea is tossing, ceaseless, in a not very far distance. The moon seduces the wave and the tide is moving like crazy. The rain drops on the ceiling above our bed, on the pond outside of the house, on the stinging nettles by the window. The whole world is raining. The whole world is drowning. There is no single place can remain dry, not even an inch.

The next morning, the rain becomes lighter, and the wind is less strong. We come down to the sitting room, having hot coffees with breakfast by the fire. It is safe and warm inside. Outside is *gloomy*. That is the word. But you don't agree. I say I don't want to go out anymore. I swear. You laugh at me. You say you love this kind of weather. You say that is what you love about the nature. Nature is powerful, and this power is beautiful.

'Shall we go to the lighthouse?' you ask.

'Lighthouse? Virginia Woolf's lighthouse?' I remember the book you gave to me.

'No, this one is more beautiful.'

'Where is it?'

'Come with me.' You stand up.

We borrow an umbrella from the old lady who owns B&B, leaving the fireplace and head to the nature again. My boots are still wet from yesterday's mud. It is a pair of city boots, losing shape here. They don't belong to this place. I should buy a pair of rubber boots, and a raincoat.

It is a long walk, through the woods and farms. After about one and half hours, we see the lighthouse. It is standing at the bottom of the hill. It faces to the sea. There is nothing else around it, not even a sheep. It feels like is built at the end of the world. We walk towards it. The lighthouse becomes closer and bigger. It is tall, thin, erect, like a young man's penis. It is totally alone, and solitude.

We sit down by the lighthouse. The seagulls are diving in the water. The waves are deep green. I imagine during the night, in the darkness, the light turns around, wiping off the mountain, the grassland, the path, the beach, the sea. I imagine the light searching, but maybe searching for nothing.

'Is any boat going to the other side of the sea?' I ask.

'Yes, but not today. Not everyday,' you say.

'Shall we ask around when there will be a boat here? So we can take the boat to see the other side.'

'You go if you want. I'd like to stay here,' you answer.

'But there is nothing here,' I say.

The current is quiet. The lighthouse is keeping something secret, a secret which I don't understand.

The city weakens your energy. But you become alive again in this place. Finding a snake or an earthworm under the grass, is more surprising than making art; seeing a dolphin dancing in the sea is more interesting than making art; watching a beam of red flowers turned into a string of beans is more satisfying than making art; listening a bumble bee sucking a bud is more pleasant than making art. I think you are born for nature. Why not stay here? Why force yourself to return London? You should stay, without considering me.

I open my notebook again, looking at my everyday's study, my everyday's effort. I see myself trying hard to put more words and sentences into blank pages. I try to learn more vocabularies to be able to communicate. I try to put the whole dictionary in my brain. But in this remote countryside, in this nobody's wonderland, what's the point of this? It doesn't matter if one speaks Chinese or English here; it doesn't matter if one is mute or deaf. Language is not important anymore. Only the simple physical existence matters in the nature.

November

pathology

pathology n scientific study of diseases

You, my English patient, keep feeling ill. I used to lie beside you, whenever you suffered from headache or bodyache. I would just stop what I was doing and come to lie beside you. But after so long, so often you get ill, somehow I run out of patience.

'Honey, I know how to cure your depression: practice yoga every morning, ride your bike every afternoon, and go swimming every evening.'

'Perhaps I just need to find the right medicine.'

'No. I don't think you can solve it under the medication way. The problem is from your Qi, your energy.'

You lie there, look at the ceiling vaguely: 'Every morning I wake up and I feel tired before I'm even out of bed.'

'That's because your illness is brought from your thoughts. You hate this society so much, and you feel so fed up with this place. You don't have any disease. You are just like your old van, old, too old, every part of the mechanic fell apart. Remember? Your white van and you, used to be so energetic.'

'I just wish I knew what it was that was wrong with me.'

'You Westerners always went to precisely name illness. But in China, we don't name all these kind of diseases. Because we think all the illness actually causes from very simple reason. If you want to solve your illness then you must start to calm your whole body, not just taking pills every time.'

'OK, tell me more.' You rise your head from the bed.

'There are three general classes of the causes of illness in Chinese medication. Internal Pathogenic Qi, External Pathogenic Qi, and Trauma. Internal Pathogenic are organ disfunction, External Pathogenic are Qi from outside the body which enter the body, and Trauma is trauma.'

'Trauma is Trauma?'

'I guess Trauma causes Qi and blood to leave the normal currents of flow. And it causes the stagnation of your inner energy. So parts of your body will be suffered from the lack of Qi. That's why you get tired everyday easily. And that's why you get headache regularly.'

'How do you know all this?' You stare at me.

'Because I am a Chinese.'

'You mean all Chinese people know about this?'

'I think so.'

'Are you serious? Even the ones who work in the Chinese takeaway on Hackney Road?'

'You can ask them, next time when we pass by,' I say.

'You know, you never tell me things like this.' Now you get up from the bed. You must feel better.

'But you never really ask me. You never really pay attention to my culture. You English once took over Hong Kong, so you probably heard of that we Chinese have 5,000 years of the greatest human civilisation ever existed in the world ... Our Chinese invented paper so your Shakespeare can write two thousand years later. Our Chinese invented gunpowder for you English and Americans to bomb Iraq. And our Chinese invented compass for you English to sail and colonise the Asian and Africa.'

You stare at me, no words. Then you leave the bed, and put the kettle on.

'Do you want some tea?' you ask.

pessimism / optimism

pessimism n tendency to expect the worst in all things

optimism n tendency to take the most hopeful view

A petal is a pessimist. A petal will fade away.

An old man's body is a pessimist, things are rotten and falling apart.

A buddhist is a pessimist in his reality, but in the end when he faces his death he is an optimist, because he has prepared for whole life to welcome the peace of death.

A farmer is an optimist, because he believes the potatoes will come out underneath the soil.

A fishman is an optimist, because he knows whatever how far he fishes, he will come back with his boat full of fish.

A pesticide is an optimist. It means sustain the good life by killing bad life.

Everyone tries to be an optimist. But being an optimist is a bit boring and not honest. Losers are more interesting than winners.

★ ★ ★

It is a quarter to six, and I am cooking dinner for you. It is already inky dark outside. I look at the clock and go back to kitchen checking the food. 6.00, then 6.10, then 6.20, then 6.30. I turn on the radio, listen to whatever I can understand. Finally it is 7.00. Since then every single minute cannot bear anymore. Paranoia takes over the kitchen. 7.30 now. You told me that you would be back home before six. Why you never on time? Are you flirting with somebody right now? Or maybe things much worse . . .

Trying to stop this painful visual imagination, I turn up the volume of the radio. Today's top news: '*A woman murdered her husband's pregnant lover after she discovered the love affair . . . She was found guilty in court this afternoon.*'

The soup is still bubbling on the fire but is nearly burnt. Murder . . . The whole world is crashed. The paranoia penetrates my body through my mind. My muscles are shaking badly, and my stomach starts aching. I am in the big nerve and I might do anything to destroy the furniture in this house, the symbols of our life together.

Love can be so pessimistic, and love can be so destructive. Love can lead a woman being lost, and in that lost world perhaps the only thing to do is leave to build a new world.

9.00, you come back home. I pour all the food into the rubbish bin. You are a bit scared seeing what I am doing. I say loudly, to myself, and to the whole house:

'Never cook food before the man comes back home!'

electric

electric adj produced by, transmitting, or powered by electricity; exciting or tense

> Hair, bosom, hips, bend of legs, negligent
>   falling hands all diffused . . . mine too
>   diffused,
> Ebb stung by the flow and flow stung by the
>   ebb . . . love-flesh swelling and deliciously
>   aching
> Limitless limpid jets of love hot and enor-
>   mous . . . quivering jelly of love . . . white-
>   blow and delirious juice,
> Bridegroom-night of love working surely and
>   softly into the prostrate dawn,
> Undulating into the willing and yielding day,
> Lost in the cleave of the clasping and sweet-
>   flesh'd day.

This is in a book from Walt Whitman, which sits on your bookshelf covered by the thick dust. But during the last two weeks it becomes my bible. I read it every day and I think I understand it.

Jelly of love. I think of you. You are like the man in Walt Whiteman's poem. I imagine you are naked by the sea, a wild landscape behind you. You are a young man with a healthy body and a free spirit. You are a simple farmer, with a natural passion. You have beautiful hips and legs and hands, and you have a strong love and sensibility to the nature. You are friends with the seagulls, the bees, the dragonflies. And you know that dolphin in the distance dancing on the sea. You walk through the fields of apple trees, and pass by the farm houses, and then down to the sea. You body carries the smell of grass and the warmth of earth to the sea water . . . I look at your reality here. How could these things being taken away from you totally? You will die. You will die. You will die like a fish without water.

The life in the past and the life at the present are very different. When I first met you, I remember you always talked and smiled. You talked about interesting things in an interesting way, and you had a charming language. You used beautiful words, funny words, sexy words, *electric* words, *noble* words. Your language was as attractive as you. But what happened? It has changed. After all these fightings, all these miseries, you don't talk as the way you did before. You just listen; listen to my words; then stop listening and think of your own world. But I can't stop talking. I talk and talk, more and more. I steal your words. I steal all your beautiful words. I speak your language. You have given up your words, just like you gave up listening. All you do is sleep, more and more sleep.

bestseller

bestseller n book or other product that has sold in great numbers

Last night I had a dream. I dreamed I was a cookery writer writing for housewifes who bored with their unimaginative life. I dreamed my book eventually exposed on the most visible and conspicuous shelfs in Waterstones. I become a bestseller who has the fame in England, Scotland, and even in Wales. My book was called *Getting To Grips With Noodles: 300 ways of Chinese cooking*. Actually, at the beginning of my dream, there were only ten recipes of cooking noodles, but in the dream I had the idea that a year has 365 days and I should write at least 300 different recipes. Rest of sixty-five days in a year people can have rice or bread or alternative food they like.

I remember the first dish in my book is called:

Dragon In the Clouds

The recipe is: thin rice noodles with fried tofu and bean sprouts in a chicken soup. So everything looks white and gentle like clouds.

And other noodles dishes in my dream are:

Red River
Mussels with spring onions in chilli noodles soup

Double Happiness
Roast duck and pork with fried noodles

Dragon Palace
Sliced eel with rice noodles in ginger soup

It's also about two-way-cooking, meaning either it can be prepared as Chinese food or it can become Italian spaghetti. For example, one can just change ginger into basil, or replace chilli to rosemary with a bit cheese, then noodles will get totally different *identity*.

End of dream, there are a group of fat middle-aged English womans talking about my book in a countryside teahouse. They are all having their afternoon teas and carrot cakes with my book opened on the table, and discuss where is the nearest Chinese shop that they can buy all the ingredients.

I wake up and I don't know where is this idea from. I guess from my hunger for Chinese food. I am longing to eat hot dumplings with fennel and pork stuffing, and I am dying for roasted duck and spicy beef. Abroad, thinking of food is everyday's obsession.

There is an important thing in the dream: I am too ashamed to use my real name on the cover of the book because I know as soon as I get famous in West, Chinese will find out immediately and make a fuss. A writer who doesn't write history or serious novels, but write about cooking noodles for English people — that would be a scandal in China. So I choose 'Anon' as my name, the person who has no name.

Getting up from the bed, I feel hungry. I have a great urge to taste those specially made noodles but, when I try remember how to cook the dream noodles, nothing comes in my head. I open the cupboard and take out a pack of instant noodles.

December

future tense

The Future Tense Sometimes when we talk about the future, we are just predicting. We are saying what we think will happen, without any reference to the present. At other times, we are really talking about the present and the future together. This happens, for example, when we talk about future actions which are already decided, or which we are deciding as we talk: making plans, promises, threats, offers, requests.

Mrs Margaret say I am no good at verbs, particularly future tense. 'Don't worry,' she says. 'It's an Asian thing. You'll get over it.'

How is 'time' so clear in the West? Is being defined by Science or by Buddha? Reincarnation, it is not past or future. Is endless loop. A circus, ending and starting is the same point.

At beginning I don't have concept of *tense* when I speak English. But now I think I understand more than before, after all our battles.

Sun Tzu, the Chinese master who lived 2500 years ago, says in the *Art of War for Executives*:

The ultimate warrior is one who wins the war by forcing the enemy to surrender without fighting any battles.

But neither of us wants to surrender to the other, and neither of us can win the battle. Neither of us is an ultimate warrior. So the battle carries on and on, as follows:

ME: 'I want future with you. A home, a house in beautiful place with you, plant some bamboos, some lotus, some jasmines, some of your favourite snowdrops.' (When I describe this, the image so strong that it must be a will from my Last Life.)

YOU: 'You can't have the future *now*. That's why it's the future.'

ME: 'I disagree. Future comes from your plan, your real action.'

YOU: 'No, that's not true. The future only comes when it comes. I don't believe in promises. How can you know the future now? You can only know the future when you get to the future.'

ME: 'Does that mean you don't want future with me?' (I look in your eyes painfully.)

YOU: 'You're always worried about the future. How can we think about getting married when we keep fighting? You're never happy with the way things are, you always want it to be different to how it is. We can't be together if you don't accept my lifestyle and realise you can't change me. You can't always want me to be different from how I am.'

★ ★ ★

You are right, I know. I can't say anything.

Again I feel like I am the wisteria vine, and I

288

can't climb and rely on my tree, because that tree is falling.

'Live in the moment!' You impose this idea on me, again.

'Live in the moment,' I repeat. Why do I have to? 'Live *in* the moment, or live *for* the moment? Maybe you only live *for* the moment. That is so hippy. I can't do that as a humble foreigner,' I fight back.

'Well, to live *in* or to live *for* the moment, that's the same kind of concept.'

'No. It is different,' I say, strongly and angrily. I recently learned what is the difference between *in* and *for* from Mrs Margaret. It is definitely a different concept.

'Love', this English word: like other English words it has tense. 'Loved' or 'will love' or 'have loved'. All these specific tenses mean Love is time-limited thing. Not infinite. It only exist in particular period of time. In Chinese, Love is '爱' (ai). It has no tense. No past and future. Love in Chinese means a being, a situation, a circumstance. Love is existence, holding past and future.

If our love existed in Chinese tense, then it will last for ever. It will be infinite.

possess

possess v have as one's property; (of a feeling, belief, etc) have complete control of, dominate

You tell me my love to you is like a possession. But how could I possess you when your world is so big? Maybe it not about possession, it more about me trying to fit into your life. I am living *in* your life. I am living inside of your body, trying to understand every single movement from your command. Every night I inhale and outhale your breath. The smells from your hair and your skin cover my hair and my skin. I know nobody in my life is as close as you.

I just hope night carry on like this, go on for ever. Hope our bodies can be always close like this, and our souls always can be side by side. I don't want the sun comes, the day comes. I know the light of day takes you away from me. Then you live in your own world, the world that has a big gap between us.

In the daytime, you stay with your sculptures, with your clay, your sand, your wax. You are making many moulds of human bodies. All the materials they lie there, quiet, with vague and unclear statements.

The conversation on the bed after we make love:

'Why you are always so interested in the body?'

'Because you will never get bored with the body.' You rub the sperms on my skin slowly, trying to dry it. 'Eating, drinking, shitting . . . The body is key to everything.'

'But why your sculptures ugly and miserable?'

'I don't think they are ugly. They are beautiful.'

'Maybe. Beautiful in ugly way. But they are always in pain.'

'That's what life is like.'

I can't agree, but I can't deny either.

'My body always feels miserable, except for when I am making love,' you say.

Your voice becomes sleepy, and you close your eyes.

I turn off the light. I stare at the darkness. I have enough thoughts to talk to the long night, alone.

christmas

Christmas n annual festival on Dec. 25 commemorating the birth of Christ; period around this time

Tomorrow is Christmas. We wake up to noises from neighbours' kitchen. They are probably arranging tables or chairs for their guests. You tell me we will stay in London until lunch, and then you will take me to see your family in the afternoon. I am curious, but also worried. Meeting your family is a big thing for me. That is again something to do with the future.

What happened to Jesus Christ at Christmas Eve? Was he hung on the cross? Did he almost reborn? We were taught when we were little that only the phoenix can be reborn. A beautiful huge bird, with the neck of a snake, the back of a tortoise, and the tail of fish. She eats dewdrops. She lives for a thousand years and, once that time is over, she burns itself in her own funeral pyre, and is born again from the ashes. Jesus must be something like a bird, the symbol of high virtue.

Winter is such a long season in England. Hackney Road is dim, dark, wet and obscure. But there is something extra which makes you and me nervous about this time. Neither you nor me kind of person likes celebrating festivals, plus I don't have any family here. Outside, neon lights are twinkling, shining like the fragile happiness.

Almost a year has passed. In the beginning, we were so passionate about each other. Now everything grows older, and covered by the dust. Every morning you go to that corner shop to buy newspaper. You sit in a small café having a breakfast and reading. You would rather read the paper outside somewhere, because you say you can't relax at home. Should I leave the house and give the space back to you?

Afternoon. We are in your white van. We are driving to the southwest of England, to Lower End Farm, the place where you grew up. The road towards the countryside is so quiet. Like a road nobody knows, as if nobody has driven through it before. It is getting darker. It is grey. The houses beside the road are all lighted. Ah, others are all happy, with their family. I hate Christmas.

I start to cry.

You look at me one moment, then look at the road. You know why I am crying. You keep quiet. Only the noise from the engine carries on.

'It will be all right,' you say.

But I don't know what all right even means.

I stop crying. I calm down a bit. It's only four in the afternoon, but the sky in countryside is already deep dark, and the rain comes with the chilly wind. The wind blows the pine trees, the grass, and the oaks in the fields. The leaves are shivering, and the branches are shaking. There must be too much wind in English's blood.

Dim and muddy, it is the road leading to your childhood . . .

That evening, you show me around the farm with torch. It is a big farm, extended to the horizon. Some sheeps or maybe cows in the distance, mooing.

There are four old womans in this house: your mother, your grandmother, your two sisters. Three cats live in this old farm house too. I wonder if these cats are all females? No man. Your two sisters, one is 42, another is 48. You told me they never get married. Maybe they get used to this old-girl-life, so they don't need or want a man anymore. Your father died long time ago, and so did your grandfather. But all womans survive.

These womans, in your family, they are all farmers. They look like they have had a hard life. Their faces, reddish on the cheeks from the chilly wind. They are simple and a little tough. They are very straightforward, and have very strong impression towards every little thing. Their questions are like these:

'Zhuang? What kind of a name is that? How do you spell it?'

'Do you watch TV, Z?'

'Z, how many hours does it take to fly from China to England?'

'Bloody hell! One billion. Are there really so many people in your country?'

They talk loudly, and laugh loudly, and chop the meat loudly in the kitchen. They remind me of my family. They are very different from Londoners.

There are about twenty silver and golden badges on the wall of dining room. These badges are hung under the photos of sheep and cows, the winners of some farming competitions. Several local newspapers are pinned on the wall, with pictures of your sisters hugging her award-winning cow. And the cow has a big badge hung on its neck too. I don't understand this competition between cow and cow.

In TV room is a huge poster about sheep. Every sheep has its different name, and they do look like very different. The one on the left is called *Oxford Down*, look like a big fat dog, but with burnt black nose and ears. The one on the right is called *Dartmoor*, with messy curly wool like a woman in hair salon having an electricity perm. The bottom one is called *Exmoor Horn* with curly horns and short body like a snow ball . . . There are no pictures of human beings. It is like a sheep museum.

I walk into the kitchen. Your mother is preparing Christmas Eve supper. I see the plates with drawing of sheep, and tea cups with the picture of cow, and the tea pot is the shape of a little goat.

Everything in the house looks *aged*, as old as your grandmother. Your grandmother is ninety-seven. She lives upstairs. You take me to say hello to her. She is skinny. She is too old to move around. Also she is too old to talk. She doesn't seem to recognise who you are.

I try to understand these four womans, with their strong accent. I can't tell if they are tough or friendly. There is a certain kind of brutal feel from your sister when she chops the meat that makes me timid. Is that one of the reasons you left your hometown, came to London, and didn't want to be with any womans when you were young?

After the supper, everybody is tired and goes to bed. We sleep on a sofabed in the living room. It is midnight. The whole farm outside is covered by a big piece of silence. No neighbours, no pub, no shop, no car, no train. It is a place far away from civilisation. It is even worse than my hometown in China. So quiet, like it's on the edge of the world. Occasionally, one or two fireworks blow in the distance. But rest of the world is as frozen as ice in the Arctic Ocean.

On Christmas morning, it starts snowing. The farm has a layer of light snow. I hope the farm is happy to receive the snow on a very special day. After a big brunch, we watch the Queen's speech on TV, then we say goodbye to your family, and hit the road again. Your mother and your two sisters are waving their hands in front of the house. When I look at them from the van I feel sad. Maybe we should stay more time here, eat the Christmas turkey they prepare all day. But you say you can't stay in there any longer. Not even one more afternoon, you say. We leave Lower End Farm behind. We leave the mud, the sheep, and the winter grass behind.

We drive all the way back to London. There is nobody in the street, not even a ghost. It is surreal. Almost too perfect.

The snow is like feathers gradually covers dirty London. The snow knows its own power. It understands how to make a city less bleak and more gentle.

We stop in a local café on Hackney Road, probably the only one open. The café owner is a foreigner, maybe from Middle East. I guess he prefers to work in café at Christmas rather than spend a lonely day on his own in his rented east London basement. There are beautiful red flowers on every table. It is a kind of green-leafs-turn-to-red-flowers. I am having fish and you are having chips. We look outside. The snow is falling from the sky. The café owner says 'Merry Christmas' to us. He must be so happy to see eventually two customers visit him on such lonely day.

January

betray

betray v hand over or expose (one's nation, friend, etc) treacherously to an enemy; disclose (a secret or confidence) treacherously; reveal unintentionally

I don't know if time takes us into its fast whirpool, or we suck time into our inner world. It feels like Christmas just yesterday, but now here comes New Year's day. Last night we made love like desperate people. And we made love again this morning. It feels everything so empty. Desperation. Or fear. We need make something unforgettable in our memory.

The only thing I love completely, without any doubt, is your body. I love it. Temperature. Softness. Forgiveness. Maybe I can let you go, but not your body.

Kissing. I hug your warmth. I think of other bodies I encountered, which I never really in love with. I start to talk.

'You know lots of things happened in that month.'

'That month?'

'Yes, that month.'

' . . . When you went Inter-Railing?'

'Yes.' I look into your eyes. I really want you to know. If we don't have much to talk anymore, maybe we can talk about that month, when you were absent with me.

'Are there things you didn't tell me?' You put out your hand touch my face.

'But you never ask me! It's like the newspaper is more interesting to you than reality. You would rather read the paper every day than talk to me.'

'So, talk to me now,' you say.

I'm annoyed again. Why everything has to be like this? Why I am always demanding? Why there is no curiosity inside your heart anymore?

'OK. I met some mans on the trip, you know.'

'What do you mean you met some men?'

'Yes, one in Amsterdam, one in Berlin, one in Venice and one in Faro . . . ' I suddenly can see all these faces. I can see that Portugal man with the missing teeth walking beside with me down to the dirty rocky beach under the highnoon's sun . . . And I can see Klaus standing in a street of Berlin waiting for the bus. Probably now he walks into a shop to buy a bottle of mineral water with red star brand.

'And?' You become serious.

'Nothing.'

'Nothing?'

'Nothing serious. Just, I had sex with a man who I only met for half an hour.'

You stare at me. Your face is frozen. There is only four centimetres between my face and yours.

'But I didn't like that experience, actually . . . ' I am a little worried to carry on this story.

There is no specific impression on your face.

Suddenly I remember a sentence I read from the bible on your shelf recently: *Father forgive*

302

them for they know not what they do.

'I thought I should let you know, even you don't ask me,' I continue. 'And in Berlin, I was very much attached to a man, whom I met on the train. He was ill at that time . . . '

Now I'm upset, but at the same time I feel relieved.

You get out from the bed and walk to the kitchen, naked. You add some water into the kettle, without any words. You put some dry mint into the tea pot. Then you stand there and wait for the water to be boiled.

'So if you didn't like it, why did you do it?'

Finally, you are angry.

'Because . . . I don't like distance.'

'So you have to have sex with a stranger?'

There is silence between us.

'Every time I thought you might be with another man,' you say, 'I thought we should leave each other.'

'Why?'

'I mean I should let you go.'

'Go where?'

'When I was your age, I was like you. I wanted to experience everything, and wanted to try all kinds of relationships, all kinds of sex. So I know what's going on inside you. If you stay with me, and I see you going with other men, I will be lost.'

Those words, I don't want to hear. You are afraid of being lost, but *I* am the person in the relationship being lost first.

'But you wanted me to travel alone!' I am crying.

'Because you are young . . . too young to be so serious with me,' you say. 'When you were away I often imagined you with other men, but then I stopped thinking about it. Even when you told me you were pregnant, I didn't think about it.'

You stand there, let the water boiling in the kettle, without move.

I feel your coldness covering this house. I am afraid of you. I am afraid of this kind of manner. It is the coldest manner in the world.

You start drinking your tea. A vegeterian shepherd pie is in the oven, the kind of English food I hate. Such a sad food. A kind of food shows how boring the life is. A kind of food without any passion.

We don't talk rest of the day.

You are doing something with your sculptures. Pouring hot wax into the mould. The shape is obscure. I am watching a New Year's TV programme, an animation about a nightingale. Oscar Wilde again, but this time it is visual and vivid. The nightingale is bleeding and dying, and the red rose is abandoned by the young man. 'Love is better than life,' the nightingale says.

Love is better than life! Even love brings death. Is this our New Year's wish?

infinity

infinity n endless space, time or number

When I was in the primary school, the mathematics teacher taught us to count until we were too tired to count anymore. The teacher said that the last number is 'infinity'. It is a number but numberless. One can count and count until the numbers become uncountable.

Infinity, it is an uncountable future.

Here, in our kitchen and bedroom, our battle is an infinity.

'Listen,' I shout. 'This is serious. I need to know if I should give up my job in China to stay here with you, or if I should go back to my country.' I look at my passort on the table.

'What is your job there?'

'Did you never know my job?'

'I never understood when you talked about a government work unit.'

'Well, I worked in a welfare office.'

'And what's that got to do with a government work unit?'

'Everybody in China has a work unit, and I don't want to lose that if I have to go back. It is a lifelong paid job. It is safe, you know. If I lose that, I have no choice except making shoes with my parents.'

'OK, whatever. You can't make decisions about a relationship just because you don't want to lose a job.'

Indecision, that's the term belongs to you. Is that why you are unhappy with your life?

'Do you want live with me for ever?' I start again. I have to. I'm too worried.

'I cannot say that. Nothing is for ever.'

'You don't believe in that concept?'

'No. Because I don't know the future, do I? I don't know what the future will be like.'

'But don't you wish you will be with me in the future?'

You are in silence for three seconds. Three seconds is very long for this question. Then you answer: 'The future will decide for you, not you for the future. You're from a Buddhist country, I would have thought you would know that.'

'OK. From now on we don't talk about future. All I know is: our Chinese live in the expectation. *Expectation*, is that the word close to *Future?* The farmers grow their rice in the spring, and they water it and expect it grow every day. The rice sprouts turn into green and the rice pole grow up taller. Then summer comes and the farmers look forward to grain growing bigger. Then the autumn harvest, and the grain becomes golden. Their expectation is nearly fulfilled, but not compelete. After the harvest they separate the straw and millet. The straw goes to the shepherd's pens or the pig's yard, and the millet goes to the market for sale. All this is so that a family can have better life in the winter and in the coming Spring Festival. In the winter they burn the roots and grass on the fields to nourish the soil for next year's re-plant. Everything is for the next step. So look this nature, life is about the expectation, but not about now, not about today, or tonight. So you can't only live in today, that will be the doom day.'

You stop listening. You are busy pouring hot wax into a mould. There are three different moulds, one is like a brain, and another one look like an eyeball, the third one is a big nipple. After wax pouring, you are waiting for it is cooled down, so you can pull the mould away from the wax.

Your pencil drawing is on the kitchen table. A drawing, lots of human organs, lie inside of a bath. Human bone, a leg, ears, lips, eyeballs, arms, intestines . . . it is almost ugly. Actually, very ugly. But also very strong. Once you said to me you think youself are ugly, though I don't feel like that. You said you are always fascinated by ugliness, ugly people, ugly buildings, ruins, rubbish.

I raise my eyes, contemplating the plastic bath you made. It sits there, silent, holding something vague, holding something heavy.

expel

expel v drive out with force; dismiss from a
school etc permanently

Today, my government work unit calls me.
Suddenly, I am dragged back to that society.

The officer in the phone say seriously, in the
Communist way: 'You have a contract with us.
We have to warn you to come back before you
do wrong things there. Don't break our rules.
Return back in one month according to the rule
in our work unit, otherwise you will be Kai Chu
(expelled) from our organisation.'

Kai Chu!

Expelled!

I am so angry that I want to throw my phone
away. A year in this country, I had almost
forgotten how stupid those Chinese rules are.
An individual belongs to the government, but
doesn't belongs to herself. Yes, I want to be
expelled. Please expel me. Please. But I also
know they just threaten me. They always
threaten the little people, in the name of the
whole nation. And you don't have a chance
against it. It is like Mao's little red book, it is
written in the *imperative* tone.

dilemma

dilemma n situation offering a choice between two equally undesirable alternatives

I read this word so many times on the paper and never understand it. Now, when think about whether I should stay here or go back China, I understand this word totally.

It is a difficult word just like what it means. Dilemma. Knowing this word, I also learn these words: *paradox, contradictory, alternative.*

'If I leave this country, or say we split up, what you will do?' I ask.

'I don't want to be with another woman.'

'Why?'

'I don't want to.'

'Why you don't want another lover?'

'I just want to be on my own.'

'Really? And you don't want to be with a man lover either?'

'No. I don't want anybody.'

'Really?' I think I don't understand you.

'Really. Look, you need me, and your love is a need. But I don't need anything, and I don't need you. That's why I can be on my own.'

You say: 'I'd like to be a monk. I want to give up everything: the city, desire, sex. Then I can be free.'

'We should let each other go,' you say to me.

'But we still love each other,' I insist. How can two lovers just decide to separate while they still in love with each other?

'We should leave each other.' You look at me, as it is said by a priest, a sober priest in the church.

Suddenly I feel that you have already made up your mind. And nothing can be changed. But I still remember that love song you sang to me before, under your fig trees in the garden. The lyrics and the melody are still wandering around in my ears:

It's the heart afraid of breaking
that never learns to dance

I think you only want the joyful part of love, and you dare not to face the difficult part of love. In China we say, 'You can't expect both ends of a sugar cane are as sweet.' Sometimes love can be ugly. But one still has to take it and swallow it.

I start to deal with my immigration papers. I have to apply for an extension of my visa. It is frustrating. I need to show my bank details to the Home Office that I have stable income to live here, but certainly I don't have any income. Everything is family supported. How much money I left in my bank? Two hundred pounds? Or one hundred and fifty pounds by tomorrow? Most importantly, I don't have any reason to stay here, except for you. And I feel confused. I want to stay but I don't know if it is the right decision. My parents' opinions now seems don't bother me very much like before. Plus, they know nothing of my life here.

I thought that you would bring everything into my life. I thought you are my Jesus. You are my priest, my light. So I always believed you are my only home here. I feel so insecure because I am so scared of losing you. That's why I want to control you, I want you are in my view always and I want cut off your extension to the world and your extension to the others.

I think of those days when I travelled in Europe on my own. I met many people and finally I wasn't so afraid of being alone. Maybe I should let my life open, like a flower; maybe I should fly, like a lonely bird. I shouldn't be blocked by a tree, and I shouldn't be scared about losing one tree, instead of seeing a whole forest.

timing

timing n the choice, judgement or control of when something should be done; a particular time when something happens

Today I read about tense again. It is a sentence from Ibn Arabi, an old sage, a very wise man living in the early thirteenth century. He said:

> *The Universe continues to be in the present tense.*

Does that mean English tense difference is just complicated for no reason? Does that mean tenses are not natural things at all? Does that mean love is a form that continues for ever and for ever, just like in my Chinese concept?

About *time*, what I really learned from studying English is: *time* is different with *timing*.

I understand the difference of these two words so well. I understand falling in love with the right person in the wrong timing could be the greatest sadness in a person's entire life.

You had all this of beautiful energy inside when I first met you in the cinema. But things have changed. All our fight, all your strugglings with London, all of that has made you look like a small dried fig fell from the tree.

In our garden, in the last several days, figs fall from the tree, the fruit tree without flowers. They didn't grow or ripen during the summer, but they can't go through winter either. They are tiny, immature, greenish, and shrinking like an old man without a happy youth. Those figs are full of small wrinkles on the skin. They look very sad. In the morning, you walk to the garden, pick up those figs from the soil, and your palms are full of dirt and pity.

I remember those days when we first met. Then, the figs grew lively. I remember you once opened a big soft fig to show me the seeds inside. It was pink and delicate inside, and you would let me suck those sweet juice . . . Now it is winter, the time of dying, our hard time.

You see those tiny figs drop from the tree to the dirt, and you pick up them one by one. You come back to the kitchen and put these tiny green round things on the table, the table which we use for chopping vegetables, the table you always read newspapers, and the table which I use to study English and do my homework every night.

One, two, three, four, five, six, seven, eight, nine, ten, eleven, twelve . . . There are seventeen tiny figs on the kitchen table now. They are quiet, obscure, plain, and anonymous. They want say something to me, but eventually they are tired. They are dried up by the seasons, just like you.

I see your beauty is being diminished, by me. Day by day. Night by night.

February

contradiction

contradiction n a combination of statements, ideas, or features which are opposed to one another; the statement of a position opposite to one already made

You always live in the middle of two realities. You want to be able to make the art work, but at the same time you don't value it. You want to be away from London, to settle down in a pure and natural place, with mountain and sea, but at the same time you are obsessed to communicate with the society.

Sometimes, we go out for a walk. We walk in the Victoria Park, or we will walk from Broadway Market Street through London Fields. Your pale face is hidden in your old brown leather jacket, and your cheeks tell the pains with no name.

Sometimes I can't help to kiss you, to soften you, to cheer you up. You walk slower than before, slow just like we are a real old aged couple. You are struggling with yourself.

'Do you want to come to China with me?' Again, I invite you. And for the last time, I invite you.

You stop walking and look at me. 'Yes. But I don't know if I want to travel anymore. I need to stop *drifting*.'

★   ★   ★

London Fields is in yellow grey. The maple trees are naked. No more children playing around. I wonder if I will be able to see this grass again, coming out in the next spring.

In Hackney Town Hall Library we sit and look at books.

Gustave Flaubert said, 'In Pericles's time, the Greeks devoted themselves to art without knowing where the next day's bread might come from. Let us be Greeks!'

I close the Flaubert book, looking at you. You are reading a book with the picture of sculptures. I keep thinking about Flaubert's words: artists should devote themself to the art, like a priest devote to God. But what is so important about art? Why it should be like a devotion?

'How come art can be more important than food?' I ask you in a little voice.

'I agree with you, actually.' You close up sculpture book. 'I don't think art is so important. But art is fashionable in the West. Everybody wants to be an artist. Artists are like models. That's why I hate it.'

You put the book back on shelf.

'But,' I protest, 'you are like a Chinese saying: *piercing your shield with your spear.* You are contradicting with yourself. You are making art too. So it means art is also a need, a necessary of expression.'

'Yes, but if I had better things to do I would give up making art. I would rather do something more solid.'

318

I'm confused.

I'd like to dedicate my life to do something serious, maybe things like writing, or painting, but definitely not making shoes. I don't care what you said about artists. I'd like to write about you, one day. I'd like to write about this country. People say one should separate one's real life from one's art work, and one should protect his real life from his fiction life. So one can has less pain, and be able to see the world soberly. But I think it is a very selfish attitude. I like what Flaubert said about Greeks. If you are a real artist, everything in your life is part of your art. The art is a memorial of the life. Art is the abstract way of his daily existence.

Again the Buddhist in my grandmother's voice tells me: 'The reality that surrounds us is not real. It is the illusion of life.'

fatalism

fatalism n belief that all events are predetermined and people are powerless to change their destinies

A film called *Saturday Night and Sunday Morning*, directed by Karel Reisz at 1960s. This is the last film we will see together. This is the last film I will see in London.

The beautiful young man in the film, played by Albert Finney. He is too beautiful for a humble working-class life. He is wild, he wants to play and to have fun. But of course he is also a trouble maker. He gets bored by having an affair with a married woman, and he doesn't want to take any responsibility. So he starts to chase young girls. But after a while he bored again with one young girl, she means nothing to him except for her brief beauty. Womans don't weigh anything in his restless heart. He is bored of physical work, and of unimaginative youth. He becomes frustrated because he gains nothing from searching for the excitements of life. His beauty decays. His youthful energy fades away by the end of the film.

Is your life a bit like him? Have you felt the same way as that young man felt about womans or family? I gaze at your back, your brown hair and your brown leather jacket. We walk along the night street in South Kensington. Again, how familiar, this is the place we first met. It has been one year.

We stop in front of a little corner shop to buy some samosa. The shop is about to close.

'So you don't think he can love that married woman?' I ask.

I am still living in the film.

'No.' You take two cold vegetarian samosa from the shopkeeper.

'And, you don't think he can love that young girl either?'

'No. None of them love each other. No love exists between them,' you comment. 'They are loveless.'

I bite the cold samosa. Ah. Loveless.

'What you will do if you were the man in the film?' I don't let you go.

'I would leave the town, just like I left Lower End Farm. Things are dead and finished in that town.'

I stop eating samosa. One more thing I need to know: 'Why you don't want to be with that young woman either? She is young, and pretty and simple. They can be together for the rest of their lifes.'

'Because she demonstrated how limited she is at the end of the film. Remember the last scene? When they sit on the hill looking down on the suburb, and she says to him that one day they will live in one of those houses? He listens to her and throws the stone down the hill.'

'Why a house, or a home, is a boring thing?'

'Because . . . '

You stop. You don't want to explain anymore. Maybe you know you are being unreasonable.

★ ★ ★

We arrive at home at midnight. The little street is dead quiet, and the house is dead cold. We are so tired; nobody wants to have further discussion. We know clearly how far we could reach if we carry on the discussion about love and life. We both give up, without saying it.

Then I realise it is indeed Saturday night and Sunday morning. A doom night and a doom morning. An absolutely doom moment in my life. There is a special delivery letter sitting on the kitchen table waiting for me. You got it this morning. My heart is racing, racing badly. No, I shouldn't open this letter. It is from Home Office.

It is you who open it. You read it, and give it to me, without any words.

There is a black stamp on the page twenty-two of my passport, from IMMIGRATION & NATION-ALITY DIRECTORATE of Home Office. It is a pentagonal stamp. Pentagon, a strange shape. Only the Pentagon near Washington has that strange shape. It is a doom stamp.

The application for my extension of UK visa has been refused.

★ ★ ★

Once you told me I am an *agnostic*, or maybe even a *sceptic*, but now I proof myself that actually I am a *fatalist*, like lots of Asian people are. The result of my visa application is in my expectation. Not because I am being a *pessimist*, just because I know there is no actual reason for both me and authority to extend this visa. I already knew this when I prepared my paperwork. I say there is no reason, I mean even you: you can't be my reason to stay in this country. And you can't save my life. You, a possible *Anarchist*, always want to be free.

I put my passport back in a drawer. I sit down, switch on the lamp and open my notebook. I look at all the words I learned in the last week. Then I look at all the words I learned since the first day I arrived in this country: *Alien, Hostel, Full English Breakfast, Properly, Fog, Filthy Water* (actually *fizzy water*, now I know) . . . So many words. So much I learned in the passed year. The vocabularies on my notebook, day by day, become more and more complicated, and more and more sophisticated.

I open a new page, a blank page; I start to write down the film title *Saturday Night and Sunday Morning*. The pen holds in my hand with the anger, and deep disappointment — the anger about my fate, the disappointment about you.

'What are you writing?' You stand in the opposite corner of the room, staring at me.

I don't want to answer.

'I know what you are writing, actually.'

You voice sounds vague. Not only vague, but also cold.

You turn your back and throw me the last

sentence before we go to bed:
'AT LEAST YOU'RE STILL LEARNING A LOT. EVEN IF EVERYTHING IS BROKEN.'
You voice horrifies me.
You leave me, and disappear into the bedroom.

race

race 1 n contest of speed; any competition or rivalry, e.g. the arms race; rapid current or channel

'Life is a race against time.' My father always says so:

'Wasting time is shameful, just like leave the grain rotten in fields.'

'An inch of time is an inch of gold, but you can't buy that inch of time with an inch of gold.'

After all these education, I believed time was the most expensive thing in the world. When I was a teenager in the middle school, I dared not waste just even twenty minutes to play around. Staring at blue sky having daydream is a fool. Sleeping on the grass under the sun is a lazy cow, without producing milk for the people. Wasting time will earn nothing back in the future. But here, in this country, people spent whole afternoon having a pot of tea, and spent hours having a piece of cheese cake, and a whole night to drink beers in the pub. If life is a race against time, why people pay so much attention on tea and cake and beer?

'You are too anxious. Try to relax. Try to enjoy life.' You say it to me, on the way back from Wales to London.

If life is a race against time, like my father and my teacher said, then life itself must be a very aggressive thing. There is no peace and no relaxation in a race. And one's life would never win anything in the end. Because whatever effort one makes, time always parallels passing the one. The one will eventually stop racing one day, let time goes by. My father is wrong, I think. People here they don't live like that.

And what about you, my Lover? Life to you seems not a race at all. Because you already decide not living in the towns and society, but living in the nature, living with the sea and the mountain and the forest. So there will be no more social struggle to you anymore. So you can achieve peace. You talk slow and walk slow, you let the time pass by you, because you don't want to be in a race. So you won't lose, in the end.

And here it comes to the fate. I met you; a man was born in the year of Rat. A rat never has a stable home, like me, born the year of the goat. Two unstable animals, two homeless things. It won't work. It is our destiny.

In China, we say: '*There are many dreams in a long night.*' It has been a long night, but I don't know if I want to continue the dreams. It feels like I am walking on a little path, both sides are dark mountains and valleys. I am walking towards a little light in the distance. Walking, and walking, I am seeing that light diminishing. I am seeing myself walk towards the end of the love, the sad end.

I love you more than I loved you before. I love

326

you more than I should love you. But I must leave. I am losing myself. It is painful that I can't see myself. It is time for me to say those words, those words you kept telling me recently. 'Yes, I agree with you. We can't be together.'

departure

departure n the action or an instance of departing

Dear Student, Welcome to London! On finishing our course, you will find yourself speaking and thinking in your new language quite effortlessly. You will be able to communicate in a wide variety of situations, empowered by the ability to create your own sentences and use language naturally.

This is what language school leaflet says. Is it true? Perhaps. Mrs Margaret tells me she is proud of me speaking English like this among her other students. When our last lesson finished, I finally pluck up my courage and run after her:

'Mrs Margaret, can I ask you a question?'

'Of course you can.' She smiles.

'Where did you normally buying your shoes?'

'Where do I normally buy my shoes?' she corrects me. 'Why? Do you like them?' She looks down her shoes. It is a coffee-colour, high-heel shoes, with a shining metal buckle in front.

'Yes,' I reply.

'Thank you. I bought them from Clarks.'

'Oh.' I remember there is a shoes shop in

Tottenham Court Road called Clarks.

Mrs Margaret intends to leave.

'You know, Mrs Margaret, my parents are shoemakers.'

'Oh, really? Well, I know China produces goods for the whole world . . . ' She smiles another time. 'Anyway, good luck with your studies. I hope to see you again.'

'Thank you.' I smile to her as well.

'By the way, it is not right to call me Mrs Margaret. You should say Mrs Watkinson, or just Margaret. All right?'

'All right, Margaret.' I lower down my voice.

'Bye.'

'Bye.'

I like her, in the end.

★　★　★

When a woman is leaving her man, when a woman finally decides her departure,

Does she still need to water the plants every day?

Does she still need to wait until the spring, until seeing the flowers come out in his garden, probably in two weeks? Or in three weeks?

Does she still need to wash his shirts, socks and jeans? Check all his pockets before washing them?

Does she still need to cook food every evening before he comes back? Soup, or rice? Or salad? Or noodles? Or just leave everything uncooked in the fridge? Like those days when he was a bachelor?

Does she still need to wash the dishes, and sweep the floor?

Does she still kiss him? When he comes back through the evening door?

Does she still prepare the hot water for him and pour refreshing bath oil in the hot water at night?

Does she still lie down beside him when he suffers migraine every two days? Or even worse, every single day?

Does she still touch his skinny body? Using her soft hand? Stroke his naked arm? His naked chest? His naked belly? And his naked legs?

Does she still want to make love with him?

Does she, or will she cry, when she feels her body needs somebody to cover it and warm it, but not this one, the one lies beside hers?

Does she, or will she say, I am leaving you, on a particular day? Or at a particular time? Or in a particular moment?

Does she, or will she hire a car or a taxi, to take all her things before he understands what's happening?

Does she, or will she cry, cry loudly, when she starts leading her head to a new life, a life without anybody waiting for her and without anybody lighting a fire for her?

★ ★ ★

The telephone rings. The Chinatown travel agency tells me my air tickets are ready to pick up. I take all my money and I put on my coat. On the way out, I pass by your sculpture. It is

330

nearly finished. All the pieces of the body lie jumbled at bottom of plastic bath.

I come out from the house, you are standing in the garden and watering the plants. You stand still, holding the hose, with your back towards me. The brown of your leather jacket is refusing me, or maybe avoiding me. I think you don't want to see me leaving. I think you are angry. Water from the hose in hard stream straight on the plants. For a long time you don't move. I am waiting. I look up at the grey sky. I want to tell you it is winter. I want to tell you maybe you don't need to water the plants today. But I don't say anything. I walk out, hesitate, quiet. When I try to close the garden's door, I hear your voice:

'Here, take these.'

I turn back. I see you pulling out a small bunch of snowdrops from the soil. You hold out those little white flowers and walk towards me.

'For you.'

I take the snowdrops. I gaze at the flowers in my hand. So delicate, they are already wilting in the heat of my palm.

Afterwards

epilogue

epilogue n short speech or poem at the end of a literary work, esp a play

Day 1

It's a big aeroplane, with so many seats, so many passengers. Air China, with the phoenix tail drawn on the side. This time, it takes me east. Which direction is the wind blowing now, I wonder? Coming to England was not easy, but going back is much harder. I look at the window and it reflects a stranger's face. It's not the same 'Z' as one year ago. She will never look at the world in the same way. Her heart is wounded, wounded, wounded, like the nightingale bleeding on the red rose.

The lights are on again. A Chinese steward smiles at me, and serves my second meal: rice with fried pork and some broccoli. It is hot, and sticky. As my body slowly digests the rice, I understand, deeply, in my bones: we are indeed separated.

People say nowadays there are no more boundaries between nations. Really? The boundary between you and me is so broad, so high.

When I first saw you, I felt I saw another me, a me against me, a me which I contradicted all the time. And now I cannot forget you and I cannot stop loving you because you are a part of me.

But, maybe all this is just nonsense, Western philosophical nonsense. We can't be together just because that is our fate, our destiny. We have no yuan fen.

Thirteen hours later, we touch down in Beijing. I spend day walking around the city. The sandy wind from the Mongol desert drags through bicycles, trees, roofs. No wonder people are much stronger and tougher here. The whole city is dusty and messy. Unfinished skeletons of skyscrapers and naked construction sites fill the horizon. The taxi drivers spit loudly on to the road through their open windows. Torn plastic bags are stuck on trees like strange fruits. Pollution, pollution, great pollution in my great country.

I call my mother. I tell her I have decided to leave my hometown job and move to Beijing. She is desperate. Sometimes I wish I could kill her. Her power control, for ever, is just like this country.

'Are you stupid or something?' she shouts at me in the telephone. 'How will you live without a proper job?'

I try to say something:

'But I can speak little bit English now, so maybe I can find a job where I use my English, or perhaps I will try to write something . . . '

She strikes back immediately: 'Writing on paper is a piece of nothing compared with a stable job in a government work unit! You think you can reshape your feet to fit new shoes? How are you going to live without government medical insurance? What if I die soon? And what if your father dies as well?'

She always threatens to die the next day. Whenever it comes to this deadly subject, I can only keep my mouth shut.

'Are you waiting for rabbits to knock themselves out on trees, so you can catch them without any effort?! I don't understand young people today. Your father and I have worked like dogs, but you haven't even woken up yet. Well, it's time you stopped daydreaming and found yourself a proper job and a proper man. Get married and have children before your father and I are dead!'

As I keep silent and don't counter her, she throws me her final comment:

'You know what your problem is: you never think of the future! You only live in the present!'

And she bursts into tears.

Day 100

During my year of absence, Beijing has changed as if ten years passed. It has become unrecognisable.

I am sitting in a Starbucks café in a brand new shopping centre, a large twenty-two-storey mall with a neon sign in English on its roof: *Oriental Globe*. Everything inside is shining, as if they stole all the lights and jewels from Tiffany's and Harrod's. In the West there is 'Nike' and our Chinese factories make 'Li Ning', after an Olympic champion. In the West there is 'Puma' and we have 'Poma'. The style and design are exactly the same. The West created 'Chanel no. 5' for Marilyn Monroe. For our citizens we make 'Chanel no. 6' jasmine perfume. We have everything here, and more.

At night, some friends take me to a Karaoke. The place is not made for me. It is for Chinese men who seek freshness when they have grown tired of their old wives. In empty rooms, young women in tight miniskirts with half naked breasts wait for loners to come and sing. The dim rooms remind me of the pubs in London: smoke, leather seats, low tea tables, loud voices and crazy laughing. I sit and listen to men singing songs like *The Long March* or *The East Is Red*.

I feel out of place in China. Wherever I go, in tea houses, in hotpot restaurants, in People's parks, in Dunkin Donuts, or even on top of the Great Wall, everybody talks about buying cars and houses, investing in new products, grabbing the opportunity of the 2008 Olympics to make money, or to steal money from the foreigner's pockets. I can't join in their conversations. My world seems too unpractical and nonproductive.

'But you can speak English, that alone should earn you lots of money! Nowadays, anything to do with the West can make money.' My friends and my relatives keep telling me this.

Day 500

I think I have received your last letter. It arrived a month and a half ago and there has been nothing since then. I don't know why.

I think maybe I will never go back to England, the country where I became an adult, where I grew into a woman, the country where I also got injured, the country where I had my most confused days and my greatest passion and my brief happiness and my quiet sadness. Perhaps I am scared to think that I am still in love with you.

But all these thoughts don't matter too much anymore. Only sometimes, when I am alone in Beijing in my flat, an obscure night, noisy construction sites outside my window, I still can feel that pain. Yes, the geography helps a lot. I know the best thing to do is to let each other go, to let us each live on a different planet, parallel lives, no more crossing over.

This is the last letter I received from you. The last.

Dear Z,

I am writing to you from Wales. I've finally moved out of London. The mountain behind my stone cottage is called Carningli. It is Welsh, it means Mountain of the Angel . . .

I brought some of our plants and the old kitchen table here. I think the sunflowers are missing you. Their heads have bowed down in shame — as if they have been punished by their school teacher — and their bright yellow petals have turned deep brown. But I think your little bamboo tree is very happy because we have had Chinese weather for the last month. Last week I planted some climbing roses outside my cottage because I thought it would be good to have more colours around.

Every day I walk through the valley to the sea. It is a long walk. When I look at the sea, I wonder if you have learned to swim . . .

Your words are soaked in your great peace and happiness, and these words are being stored in my memory. I kiss this letter. I bury my face in the paper, a sheet torn from some exercise book. I try to smell that faraway valley. I picture you standing on your fields, the mountain behind you, and the sound of the sea coming and going. It is such a great picture you describe. It is the best gift you ever gave me.

The address on the envelope is familiar. It must be in west Wales. Yes, we went there together. I remember how it rained. The rain was ceaseless, covering the whole forest, the whole mountain, and the whole land.

Acknowledgements

The author wishes to thank Rebecca Carter,
Claire Paterson, Beth Coates, Alison Samuel,
Rachel Cugnoni, Suzanne Dean, Toby Eady,
Clara Farmer, Juliet Brooke, and all the others
who have followed this book on its journey.

341

We do hope that you have enjoyed reading this large print book.

Did you know that all of our titles are available for purchase?

We publish a wide range of high quality large print books including:
Romances, Mysteries, Classics
General Fiction
Non Fiction and Westerns

Special interest titles available in large print are:
The Little Oxford Dictionary
Music Book
Song Book
Hymn Book
Service Book

Also available from us courtesy of Oxford University Press:
Young Readers' Dictionary
(large print edition)
Young Readers' Thesaurus
(large print edition)

For further information or a free brochure, please contact us at:
Ulverscroft Large Print Books Ltd.,
The Green, Bradgate Road, Anstey,
Leicester, LE7 7FU, England.
Tel: (00 44) 0116 236 4325
Fax: (00 44) 0116 234 0205

GETTING RID OF MATTHEW

Jane Fallon

What to do if Matthew, your secret lover of the past four years, decides to leave his wife Sophie (and their two daughters) and move into your flat — just when you're thinking that you might not want him anymore . . . PLAN A: tell him you have a moustache wax every six weeks; stop having sex with him; don't brush your teeth or your hair. PLAN B: give yourself a false identity; meet and befriend Sophie; actually begin to like Sophie; befriend Matthew's children — unsuccessfully; watch your whole plan go horribly wrong . . . Getting rid of Matthew isn't as easy as it seems, but along the way Helen will forge an unlikely friendship, find real love and realize that nothing ever goes exactly to plan.

LOVE & DR DEVON

Alan Titchmarsh

Dr Devon is not the only man with woman trouble. Tiger Wilson has been married (perhaps a little too comfortably) for thirty years, and Gary Flynn is a serial womaniser who refuses to settle down. But during one month in spring they are all about to have their lives turned upside down — and not just by women . . . In seeking to add a little excitement to their lives, they get more than they bargained for. They all have their secrets, and they are all exposed to danger. The result? Death, intrigue and passion. Will Dr Devon find true love and live happily ever after? Or will the bitter pill of reality prove a fly in the ointment of his dreams?

DEAR JOHN

Nicholas Sparks

When John meets Savannah, the attraction is mutual and love quickly flourishes. John is ready to make some changes — always the angry rebel at school, he has enlisted in the army, not knowing what else to do with his life. Now he's ready to turn over a new leaf for the woman who has captured his heart. But the events of 9/11 will change everything . . . John is prompted to re-enlist and fulfil what he feels is his duty to his country. But he and Savannah are young and their separation is long. Can their love survive the distance? Years later, when John returns to North Carolina and the woman he left behind, he realises he must now make the hardest decision of his life . . .

BABY PROOF

Emily Giffin

Claudia and Ben seem to be the perfect couple. Ever since their first date, when they discovered that neither saw children in their future, the path of their relationship seemed destined to succeed. They envisage a life filled with freedom, possibility and exploration. Claudia and Ben are together because they want to be, not because children are caging them with eighteen years of obligation. But things don't always stay the same. Their best friends get pregnant, and suddenly Ben changes his mind. He does want children after all. The couple are at a crossroads: Ben and Claudia face the emotional consequences of an impossible dilemma and Claudia must decide what she wants most in life.

CLOSER TO HOME

Erin Kaye

Kath left Northern Ireland for Boston and established a new life there, with a highly successful career, a condo, and a lovely relationship. Yet her world, and her heart, are suddenly shattered: her man Carl turns out to be married, and then she hears her father has died . . . Kath returns to Ireland and throws herself into restoring her family's fortunes. But then Carl turns up and Kath faces a dilemma — he's left his wife, and has come to try and win her back . . .

ONE SUMMER

Rachel Billington

K, an English painter, has returned from
Chile to attend the wedding of a girl he once
loved to the point of obsession. But the
wedding has been postponed. He drives to
an hotel — a place he'd visited many years
before — opens a bottle of champagne
and, with it, a door to the past. When K first
saw Claudia fourteen years earlier, he fell
instantly and dangerously in love. He was
already married and Claudia, a schoolgirl,
was twenty-four years younger than him;
their love proved to be ultimately destructive
and tragic. Now K returns to find Claudia
facing a very different future. But the past
cannot easily be banished. As they are
inexorably drawn towards each other, long-
unanswered questions surface.